# The
# South-West
# *Highway Atlas*
# for 1675

### Paul White

This book is a tribute to
John Ogilby's *Britannia* Volume the First

Tamar Books · Launceston

First published 2005 by Tamar Books,
an imprint of Bossiney Books Ltd
Langore, Launceston, Cornwall PL15 8LD
www.bossineybooks.com
ISBN 1-899383-82-4

**British Library Cataloguing-in-Publication Data**

A catalogue for this book is available from the British Library.

**Acknowledgements**

The prints on pages 49 and 137 are reproduced by kind permission
of the Royal Institution of Cornwall.

I am particularly grateful to my wife Jane, who has tolerated many a journey
which should have taken two hours, but instead took four, as we traced
Ogilby's routes along lanes scarcely wide enough for the car.

Printed in Great Britain by R Booth Ltd, Mabe, Cornwall

# Contents

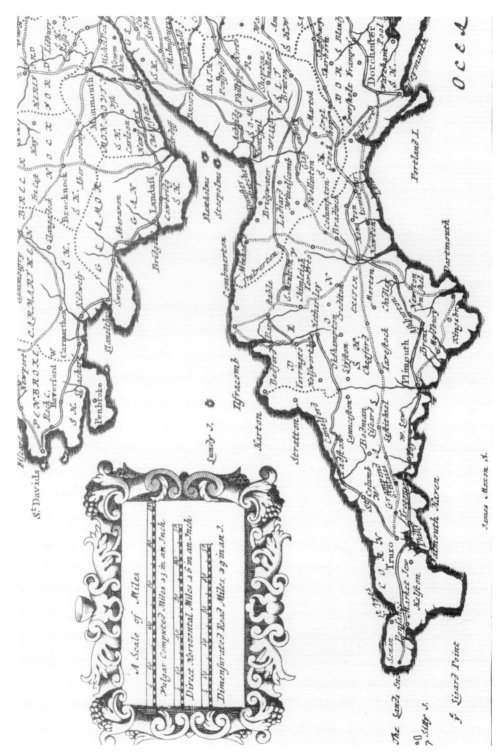

*Ogilby's key map showing which roads he included*

# Introduction

This book is the unexpected result of a casual thought some years ago. What did the roads of Devon and Cornwall actually look like before the improvements effected by the turnpike trusts, which were established after 1750? The earliest English turnpike was set up in 1663, at Wadesmill in Hertfordshire, so it had taken nearly a hundred years for this revolution in road financing, and much later in road construction, to reach the West Country.

I had read Celia Fiennes, whose travels in late Stuart England are recorded in *Through England on a Side-saddle*. She had found the Exeter to Plymouth road so narrow that it was scarcely possible for two laden horses to pass each other, except at infrequent passing places, and the conditions were even worse in Cornwall. Between the bridge at Looe and the ferry at Bodinnick:

> I met with more enclosed ground, and so had more lanes and a deeper clay road, which by the rain the night before had made it very dirty and full of water in many places; in the road there are many holes and sloughs wherever there is clay ground, and when by rains they are filled with water, it is difficult to shun danger. Here my horse was quite down in one of these holes full of water, but by the good hand of God's providence which has always been with me ever a present help in time of need, for giving him a good strap he flounced up again, though he had gotten quite down his head and all, yet did retrieve his feet and got clear off the place with me on his back.

I soon found other travellers' accounts and early maps, particularly Robert Morden's map of Devon in 1695, the first map of the county to show the road network with any degree of accuracy – but at too small a scale to identify the old line with precision. The first large scale map of Devon, at one inch to the mile, was published by Benjamin Donn in 1765. By that time a number of roads were already 'turnpiked, or projected to be so'; the map is highly informative but the process of modernisation had already begun.

Cornwall, on the other hand, was the first county in England (except for the rather less challenging Rutland) to be mapped at one inch to the mile, by Joel Gascoyne whose work was published in 1699. A facsimile edition by the Devon and Cornwall Record Society was issued in 1991, with an introduction by W L D Ravenhill and O J Padel, and this really does show the ancient routes.

But the very first accurate survey of roads in the West Country, along with the rest of England and Wales, was published by John Ogilby in his *Britannia* of 1675. Ogilby surveyed only the 'post roads', which were the highways not the byways, and certainly not the entire seventeenth century network. His published work includes some 7000 miles (of which about 800 miles appear in the present book) but Ogilby claimed he had surveyed three times that, and Robert Morden, whose map of Devon in 1695 I had first been using, seems to have had access to Ogilby's unpublished data.

It was not long before I discovered that by using these sources it is possible to trace the precise line of many of our ancient roads on a modern map, and even – to my amazement and excitement – that most of them are still there in the modern landscape. I had expected that all traces would have disappeared under eighteenth century coaching roads and early twentieth century tarmac, but this is not the case. Later replacements often left them intact.

I hope that this book will encourage readers to explore for themselves, in maps and on the ground, this ancient network of roads which in some cases probably date back thousands of years. The detective work involved is great fun in its own right, but the real delight, for me, has been the extraordinary character of some of the old routes. These really are the roads that time forgot: in some spots it is hard to believe one is in the 21st century. Exploring these roads will take you to some charming places, by definition unspoilt, since the busy world decided to bypass them several centuries ago.

Many can be explored by car, since they are country lanes – often rather narrow even by the standards of single-track roads, so beware if you don't enjoy rural driving. From time to time you will have to divert when they become bridleway or footpath, and rejoin them later. A mountain bike might be the ideal transport for some sections, but you will inevitably come across footpaths and stiles.

Some sections might be described as 'green lanes'. May I at this point explain why I shall not be using that term and why I regard it as misleading for anyone attempting to understand landscape history. It may possibly be of use to planning authorities as a label for a linear piece of land with or without a right of way, and it is certainly a helpfully emotive term to persuade local councillors not to permit building over a favourite dog-walk, but it is devoid of historical meaning.

The line of an ancient road may well, in the course of ten miles, be represented today by a main road, a country lane with grass growing down the middle, a private farm track, a well-hoofed bridleway, a theoretical but unused footpath and a pair of old hedgebanks running across grazing land. Historically it was all one highway but only the bridleway section might be considered 'a green lane'.

Conversely, 'green lanes' may be of any period from Neolithic to Victorian, and may have varied in purpose from highway to drove road to mine access track – in other words they may have nothing in common except a grassy surface.

Not infrequently an Ogilby road appears as a 'RUPP', a 'road used as public path'; this is an unfortunate legal status, as idiotic off-roaders may claim they have a right to drive along it, on the grounds that it always has been a right of way and driving has never been banned. Such 'roads' were of course made for people on foot or horseback, long before wheeled vehicles of any kind were in use in the West Country: RUPPs need better protection.

## West Country roads in 1675

What, then, were our 'roads' like in 1675? The concept of a road (or, to use the older term, 'way') was quite different at that time: it implied a right-of-way, a route, rather than any particular surface or structure. If there was a natural or man-made obstruction, the traveller had a right to find a way round it, even over private land. We would not describe them as roads at all, in the modern sense. More than a century later, in 1796, in *The Rural Economy of the West of England*, William Marshall observed:

> The roads of West Devonshire [he could equally have said 'of the West Country' in general] are, at present, most remarkable for their steepness. Less than half a century ago, they were mere gullies, worn by torrents in the rocks; which appeared as steps, in staircases, with fragments lying loose in the indentures. Speaking with little if any latitude, there was not, then, a wheel carriage in the district; nor fortunately for the necks of travellers, any horses but those which were natives of the county.
>
> At length, however, good turnpike roads are formed, between town and town, throughout this quarter of the island; and most of the villages have carriage roads open to them; though many of these by-roads, as yet, are narrow and abound with steeps. In Devonshire, as in other mountainous countries, the first inhabitants crossed the hills, on foot, in straight forward paths. When horses came into use, the same tracks were pursued; and some of them have continued in use to the present time.

On a brief excursion into Cornwall, he found that:

> The roads are of stone, and in some parts extremely well kept. The gates few and the tolls moderate. Toll roads are now formed between

most or all of the market towns. The roads of Cornwall were
formerly very rough and dangerous, especially across the open
heaths, among the mines! yet in the first introduction of them in this
country, obstinate riots took place... The road in general is good.
For a considerable way the stones are covered with a kind of rough
sand, or small gravel, apparently the loose material of which granite
is composed; making an admirable road...

The [Cornish] roads, their unlevelness apart, are among the
best in the kingdom. The towns substantial and neat. The
accommodations, equal to anything met with, out of the great roads.

As will be made apparent later, Marshall was observing our roads at a part-way stage in their improvement under the turnpike trusts, but his comments on their earlier condition are no overstatement.

Ogilby's maps make an important distinction between enclosed roads, which he shows by a continuous line, and unenclosed roads, shown with a broken line. Unenclosed roads led across open land, sometimes good pasture land but more often open moorland with 'sloughs' which were liable to cause deep despondency at certain times of year.

On a little travelled route, the track was sometimes uncertain. With no signposts, it was easy enough to get lost even in good weather, but a snowfall could be life threatening. Whilst on Gascoyne's Cornwall map of 1699 a track is shown across Bodmin Moor on the line of today's A30, only local carriers chose to go that way until the turnpike was built. John Wesley, that intrepid traveller, made annual visits to Cornwall. On his first visit, he got totally lost 'in the middle of the first great pathless moor beyond Launceston' and was only rescued by hearing the Bodmin curfew bell. The following year, 1744, he had to be guided across the moor through snow-drifts. After that he avoided the moor for the next 25 years – until 1769, year one of the turnpike.

Ogilby himself totally ignores the A30 route. He does give us a Dartmoor crossing – the post road from Chagford to Tavistock which gives us the name Postbridge – but most travellers chose to go round rather than over Dartmoor, just as they do today.

Early travellers often commented that more roads were enclosed in the West Country than elsewhere. This did not necessarily mean the land through which they passed was enclosed agricultural land – though this may have been the case, especially in Cornwall where enclosure was well in hand by Tudor times. They were simply saying that there were hedgebanks on either side of the road to prevent flocks and herds which might be driven along the road from straying into neighbouring pasture land.

Long distance movements of stock were very common – for example in Saxon times nearly every one in Devon had the right to summer pasture for their animals on Dartmoor. The technical name for this pattern of farming is transhumance, and in Saxon times roads may well have been more used for this purpose than for trade as we know it.

The very earliest surviving Devon roads are on Dartmoor, dating from around 1750 – but 1750 BC rather than AD! Just like many of Ogilby's roads 3500 years later, they consisted of a stone wall or hedgebank, probably surmounted by a thorn hedge, on either side of a track about 8 feet wide. They have survived on Dartmoor because the higher land has been so little used in subsequent centuries. Probably similar tracks existed across much of Devon and Cornwall; some at least of Ogilby's roads and of our existing country lanes will have originated in the Neolithic or the Bronze Age.

William Marshall was quite correct when he said that 'the first inhabitants crossed the hills, on foot, in straight forward paths'. It is absurd to imagine that the Romans invented straight roads! All roads, at whatever time in history, developed or were planned to be as direct as possible, though sometimes geographical features or land ownership dictated otherwise. However, even an old straight track, if unsurfaced, inevitably acquires a few wiggles as travellers avoid muddy sections or fallen trees. By the end of the Bronze Age most of our present agricultural land had been cleared and settled (some of it reverting temporarily to the wild in later times). New routes had to respect property rights. You could not expect to make a new track through the next village's cornfields without causing conflict – unless, of course you had an army to explain your decision, as the Romans did, hence their straight roads, or could force an Enclosure Act through Parliament, thus enabling the powerful members of the community to dictate to the weaker.

In 1675 the highways which Ogilby surveyed still tended to stick to the ridges, as they had since prehistoric times, then descended steeply to cross river valleys by a ford or clapper bridge and ascended as quickly as possible on the other side. The maximum gradient acceptable to walkers is about 1 in 3, say 30%. After that we prefer to zig-zag. Such gradients are also acceptable to riders, I am told, provided that there is good surface grip – which was not the case when bare rock was exposed.

Earlier I quoted William Marshall from 1796: 'Speaking with little if any latitude, there was not [in 1750] a wheel carriage in the district; nor fortunately for the necks of travellers, any horses but those which were natives of the county.' I am told that the Dartmoor and Exmoor pony breeds are still renowned for their sure-footedness, as were the Cornish 'Goonhillies', and these and other horses used locally both for riding and carriage of goods were probably not shod. In the 21st century, leaving horses unshod is apparently once again considered good practice unless a horse is going to wear down its hooves on metalled roads, as the natural hoof gives more grip than a shoe. Early visitors remarked on how the local horses were much better suited to the conditions than their own expensive mounts, and how difficult it was to find a skilled farrier in the West Country. There was less need for farriers.

Enclosure of a road by hedgebanks on either side concentrated all traffic into a narrow strip. Medieval statutes insisted the road surface should be eight feet wide, but in north Devon a mere four feet seems to have been the norm by the eighteenth century, according to Leonard Jackson's *Roads and Bridges of the Torridge Valley* (an interesting book by a retired road engineer, self-published in 2003 and available from the Mole and Haggis Bookshop in Great Torrington).

The concentration of hooves churned up the surface, as it does today on bridleways near riding stables. On a slope the track soon became a water-course after rain and developed into a 'holloway'. If the hedge-trees were allowed to grow up, the sun never reached the road-surface; the road became a leafy tunnel, damp underfoot even in summer. None of this is speculation: if you walk in the Cornish or Devon countryside, you will soon find examples of these holloways, though fortunately most are less frequented by horses nowadays so walking is easier than it was. Some have become mere double rows of trees, separated by undergrowth impenetrable by all except small boys.

Even in open country, and on the flat, you will find holloways. Perhaps it happened naturally: but such road maintenance as there was consisted of tossing the mud to the sides, so that it created banks rather like the 'levees' which form beside a meandering river as a result of floods. Consisting of top-soil and horse manure, the banks soon flourished with vegetation.

Road repair in the Middle Ages had been the responsibility of the land-owners through whose territory the road passed. Vast tracts were owned by the Church, and the Church had a greater interest than anyone else in the maintenance of a functional road network, because it was in effect a massive multinational business. Its abbeys in particular dominated commerce across the whole of Europe. It needed the communications, and it had the incentive to apply some of its resources to road maintenance and to the building of bridges. Indulgences might be granted to those who contributed generously to bridge building. Many West Country bridges were constructed with church funding in the century prior to the dissolution of the monasteries in the 1530s.

The suppression of the monasteries, and the dispersal of their estates to Henry VIII's supporters, had an unforeseen effect on the roads. Whilst the production of each estate in agricultural and manufactured goods did not fall, and may well have risen, the new breed of landowners looked to their individual profits; collectively it would have been in their interests to pay for the wider communication network, but they never saw it that way – though they did see a benefit in shuffling off their responsibilities into the public domain. In 1555 a statute (passed by a parliament dominated by landowners) transferred responsibility for road maintenance from landowners to the local parishes, rather than to a larger administrative unit such as the county. The county was required to crack the whip over the parishes.

This might have been equitable for remote parishes where all the traffic was internal, but was highly unfair on those which had a major route passing through, and on those where a major industry (particularly forestry and perhaps also mining) caused rapid destruction of the road surfaces. With the best will in the world, such parishes could not have coped. It seems that very few parishes even tried, and there were constant but ineffective attempts from the county authorities to force them to obey the law.

The problem was twofold. The financial structure was woefully lacking, but even if a parish had wanted to create and maintain top quality roads it would have lacked the expertise to do so. And there was no provision at all for building new roads. It would not have been beyond the wit of sixteenth and seventeenth century engineers to build and maintain passable roads, but there was no market for road engineers so the profession simply did not exist.

Central government took no responsibility even for the most major roads; indeed that seems not to have occurred until the Trunk Road Act of 1936.

Bridge provision on most roads, from 1530 to 1880, was the responsibility of the county, and they were also obliged to maintain the road for 100 yards to either side of a 'county bridge'. This limit is sometimes indicated by a stone about three feet high, with a letter 'c'. Few new bridges were built, but compared to road maintenance the system worked well. Ogilby's maps show, however, that 'rills' sometimes crossed the road without bridges or culverts. These minor streams were forded, so travellers on foot expected to get their feet wet. After heavy rainfall and without drainage, the loose surface of the 'road' must easily have been washed away. This is why there were so few roads along major river valleys: apart from the river itself flooding, in the absence of culverts the tributary streams crossing the road would have washed its surface into the river.

So the roads Ogilby surveyed were frequently narrow, often 'holloways' which might be overgrown by their hedges and of a tunnel-like character, and churned up by the hooves of strings of packhorses, each laden with a pair of panniers ('seams') which might contain manure, black tin, sea sand, woollen cloth or cider apples. For a rider, meeting such a train of pack animals must have been rather like meeting a tractor or milk lorry on a single track road today – frustrating. But at least there were as yet no ruts, because there were no wheeled vehicles to make them.

## How ancient were Ogilby's roads?

Archaeological evidence about roads is minimal; they are rarely excavated because the cost would outweigh the academic benefit. 'Finds' by which a road might be dated would be highly scattered, unlike an inhabited site where people lose things every day, so it might be necessary to excavate a great length of road before finding a single item by which to date it – and then, what would we have learned? At best only the date of one short stretch.

Roads of bridleway standard had existed since the Neolithic period, when people began to settle and farm, around 4500 years ago. No doubt the network changed over the millennia, and it was certainly extended as new needs arose, for example as new settlements were made or mineral resources exploited. As long as most of the land was unenclosed, such roads followed the route a walker would take today over open ground with no visible paths, such as Dartmoor – direct, except that high ground is preferable because low ground may be boggy or subject to flooding. Individual walkers will take slightly different routes, according to inclination and seasonal conditions, but will converge at river crossings for a ford or stepping stones.

The Romans made little lasting impact west of Exeter, apart from a road towards Newton Abbot and a couple of other short stretches. Any Roman with business further west would have taken to the sea and rivers, or used the ancient trackways as the natives did. The existence of a Roman 'milestone' in Tintagel church is certainly not proof of a 'Roman road' in the area, though a list of garbled place names in the *Ravenna Cosmography* (eighth century) may imply a route from Tintagel via North Tawton to Exeter. By Ogilby's time the Roman influence on the road network in Devon and Cornwall was very limited. However, in East Devon some short Roman stretches seem to have been in use which have since been abandoned. An analysis of Ogilby could show to what extent Roman roads were utilised elsewhere in Stuart times.

The Saxons had a category of road called a hare-path, *here-paeth*, which is translated as 'army road'. It implies a long-distance route, and it was doubtless of use to civilian travellers as well as the army. The name has survived at a number of places in the West Country and also appears in Saxon charters, since such roads were often used as boundaries to land-holdings.

In the Saxon and later medieval period we can, I think, assume that new roads were created as the need arose: it was, after all, only a matter of a succession of travellers on foot or horseback going the same way and beating a path! Continuous undisputed usage created a legal right of way. As more of the wasteland came back into use, new paths might need to take an indirect line around fields. By the thirteenth century there are records of landowners being required to clear ditches alongside the roads across their land, though such obligations had probably existed in previous centuries.

Did the roads of Ogilby's time follow the same line as these older roads? The evidence does not exist to answer that question with any certainty, but probably the majority of Ogilby's roads broadly followed very ancient routes, though their exact course might have varied over the centuries.

If you want to understand more about prehistoric and medieval roads, I can recommend the chapter on 'Routeways' in Richard Muir's *The New Reading the Landscape* (University of Exeter Press, 2000), which is a superb undergraduate level introduction to 'fieldwork in landscape history'.

## The subsequent history of roads

The history of roads after Ogilby's time becomes far clearer and is important for an understanding of what has survived from the ancient network.

It was already obvious in the seventeenth century that the roads were inadequate, but Stuart government was always under-funded (except for the maintenance of favourites or mistresses) and in any case roads were seen as a local rather than a national problem.

The solution, ultimately, was to lie in the Turnpike Trust system. An Act of Parliament would establish a trust, to be controlled by local landowners and prominent townspeople, which could raise money from local people at a good rate of interest, invest in improvements and then maintenance, and be permitted to charge a toll on all traffic. The idea was slow to take off: although the Wadesmill trust was established in 1663, there were only seven trusts by the end of that century, and no West Country trust was established until the 1750s. After that, the system began to be adopted very rapidly, in the West Country as elsewhere.

The trusts were mostly town based. Their business was not to look after an inter-town highway, but to facilitate travel into the town from all directions around it. The mileage in their charge varied from 3 to 178, and in the peak years of the 1820s, before the Railway Age made roads all but obsolete for three generations, 1100 trusts in England cared for 25 000 miles of road. Exeter was one of the largest trusts, caring for 150 miles.

The expectations of the eighteenth century trustees were limited. They took existing roads and attempted to improve the surfaces. The trustees were the wealthier members of local society, squires and merchants, the people most likely to own a carriage or aspire to one, or to use wheeled transport in the farms or businesses they owned. Making the roads passable for wheeled transport was a priority. This sometimes involved making a new line for the road, where the gradient was exceptionally steep, but in the early decades their activities were for the most part confined to the repair of potholes and spreading some broken stones and gravel – superficial work in every sense. There was no one to advise them how to do the job properly. Many of the turnpike roads in 1800 remained in terrible condition: now they carried wheeled vehicles, so ruts which might be several feet deep became a serious hazard.

It is understandable that the turnpiking of roads was widely unpopular. If you were a smallholder who just wanted to take your horse, with its panniers, to market once a week, you would not appreciate suddenly having to pay for the privilege of using a road which had been toll-free since prehistory – still less so if the journey was no easier than it had been before the turnpike. Rioting and attempts to avoid or cheat the system were relatively common.

It was not until the end of the Napoleonic Wars that Telford and Macadam began to have an impact on the general standards of road-building. Both applied scientific principles and systematic procedures to the task, and Telford in particular was associated with the building of new roads. The turnpike trusts' own expectations of what they should be able to achieve were given a massive jolt and many major routes were substantially realigned. The Exeter-Plymouth route is a good example: 14 miles were realigned following a report by the surveyor James Green in 1819. At long last, travellers ceased to follow in the hoofprints of Celia Fiennes.

At the same time, engineering knowledge allowed new roads to be built into the sides of the main river valleys, and money was made available for cuttings and embankments. Comparing the results of this work with Ogilby's roads has made me appreciate how very impressive it was. Then, just as the roads reached a decent standard and a massive coaching industry had established itself – strong enough to see off the threat of steam road vehicles, a Cornish invention – the Railway Age began. It took a long time to spread to the remoter parts of Devon and Cornwall, where both the hills and the sparse population made all transport initiatives speculative, whether road or rail, but road building inevitably slowed to a halt even where the railway had not yet reached: roads were yesterday's technology.

It was during the period from 1815 to 1840 that the problem of gradients was finally tackled. An article on 'Roads' in the *Encyclopaedia Brittanica* 11th Edition, published in 1911 when horse transport was still the norm and the writer ruminates on the possible usefulness of a new material called tar macadam, sums up the thought which had gone into the gradient question:

> [Gradients] should be as easy as practicable, having regard to the country to be traversed, and it is desirable that there should be a ruling gradient than which none should be steeper. On the level macadamized road in ordinary repair the force which the horse has to put forth to draw a load may be taken as one-thirtieth of the load. But in going uphill the horse has also to lift the load, and the additional force to be put forth on this account is very nearly equal to the load drawn, divided by the rate of gradient. Thus on a gradient of 1 in 30 the force spent in lifting is one-thirtieth of the load, and in ascending the horse has to expend twice the force required to draw the load on a level. In descending, on the other hand, on such a gradient, the vehicle when once started would just move of itself without pressing on the horse. A horse can without difficulty exert twice his usual force for a time, and can therefore ascend gradients of 1 in 30 on a macadamized surface without sensible diminution of speed, and can trot freely down them. These considerations have led to 1 in 30 being generally considered as the ruling gradient to be aimed at on first-class roads, though 1 in 40 has been advocated… All unnecessary rises and falls should be avoided, but a dead level is unfavourable for drainage and on this account 1 in 100 is the flattest gradient that is desirable.

There are many more pages in the article of expert if ponderous advice on road building and maintenance, just as the whole question of road building was once again rising on the agenda. The ruling classes were acquiring motor cars, and demanding that the roads should allow them to travel safely (and without a dustcloud) at far higher speeds than horse-drawn traffic. Yet more changes to the network were just around the corner: in another 50 years, new roads would be taking over abandoned railway tracks to form dual carriageways, and it was the railways which would seem to be obsolete.

The result of gradient alleviation in the West Country is seen at its most interesting in the curvaceous roads which climb out of the Tamar valley into

Devon, especially between Gunnislake and Tavistock, where the straight line of the old road persists as steep minor road and footpath, across which the 'modern' A390 winds backwards and forwards. G K Chesterton famously said that the rolling English drunkard made the rolling English road: the truth is it was the needs of the rolling English stagecoach.

Contemporaneously with the turnpike revolution, there was an increase in enclosure. It affected Cornwall and Devon less than many other regions, because more land had already been enclosed, but where a parish was the subject of an Enclosure Act, the 'roads' of the parish as well as the land ownership were subject to rationalisation – usually at the hands of the wealthiest landowners. Old rights of way were extinguished and new roads might be cut across the landscape, typically in straight swathes 40 ft wide with a carriageway of 20 ft. A road which had taken an indefinite route over a common would be given a precise line and hedged in. Usually it is that straight, hedged line which survives.

Another source of change was the development of landscaped parks. Roads were often diverted so as not to interfere with a gentleman's 'prospect'.

For someone tracking Ogilby's routes, the significance of these huge changes lies in what happened to the ancient roads during the great period of road improvement and enclosure, from 1750 to about 1840. Some were upgraded in the first phase of turnpikes (perhaps with a short stretch of new road round the head of a valley, where the old road had plunged directly across a stream) but were totally replaced in the second phase; these often survive as single track lanes. Some, however, became obsolete right at the start of the period: they may have disappeared entirely, but many were preserved as rights of way and are still there to be explored and enjoyed today. Local historians will probably be able to follow such changes in detail by the use of turnpike trust records, tithe maps, and other records.

## The man who put roads on the map

Map-making, and surveying generally, had become important activities by the beginning of the seventeenth century, and there had been many maps of English counties published. Whilst they featured rivers, towns and gentlemen's houses, strange to say they did not include a single road! During the Civil Wars (1642-49) armies and individual soldiers had blundered about without usable maps, attempting in many cases to draw their own as an aid to colleagues who might follow them. Why such a vital feature was omitted seems a total mystery. But John Ogilby decided to put it right.

He was an extraordinary man, and his career equally so. He was born in

1600, the son of a dancing master, was employed by the Earl of Strafford in Ireland where he rose to be Master of the Revels, and later owned a Dublin theatre. Strafford came to a sticky end in 1641; the Civil War started in 1642 and there was little demand for theatrical entrepreneurs. Ogilby's career was in ruins; somehow he ended up in Cambridge (not the obvious place for a Royalist, since it was a Puritan stronghold) where he either learned or brushed up his Latin and started a new career as a translator and publisher.

When Charles II came to the throne, Ogilby was employed on the Coronation masque, and moved as a publisher to Whitefriars in London, where he built up stock valued at over £3000 – a huge sum. He lost all this stock and his house in the Great Fire. So he rebuilt his house and started on yet another career, this time as a cartographic publisher. He had himself accredited as 'His Majesty's Cosmographer' and at the age of 69 came up with the idea of a multi-volume *Geographical Description of the Whole World*, starting with three volumes about Britain. Fortunately for us he was a realist, and put all his efforts into the initial volume, ultimately published as:

*Britannia, Volume the First*
or an illustration of the
Kingdom of England
and Dominion of Wales
By a geographical description
of the Principal Roads thereof
actually admeasured and delineated in a century of
whole-sheet copper *sculps*
accommodated with the Ichnography of the several cities and capital towns
and compleated by an accurate account of the
more remarkable passages of antiquity
together with a novel discourse of the present state

Blurb-writing was an art in its infancy. The scale of 'Volume the First' makes it a breath-taking project in its own right. Ogilby engaged surveyors, armed them all with compasses, theodolites and trundle wheels ('wheel dimensurator' was his term), established a house style and sent them off to distant corners of the kingdom to walk and map some 20 000 miles of road, asking the locals where the side roads went to and what the various streams and rivers were called. What's more, they actually did it. They came back with enough information to produce Ogilby's great work, which was published in 1675, the year before he died. The subsequent volumes were never published, there being no other publisher in London at that time with the energy and passion to see such a project to completion.

Two of Ogilby's innovations need comment. Firstly the strip map format, which made possible coherent mapping of an entirely linear feature without bothering to survey the areas to either side. When I was a child in the 1950s, I remember my father sending off for strip maps from the AA which were quite clearly a descendant of Ogilby's format.

Then there is his use of what would become known as the Statute Mile. Until his time, there was no standard length for the mile – each county had its own version, and there were even two national standards: the Long Mile (2428 yards) was the more common, but the mile of 1760 yards was sometimes used. Ogilby's work was so influential that all the other lengths of mile fell out of use.

When Celia Fiennes says she travelled '24 long miles' from Ashburton to Plymouth, she is assumed by some commentators to be using the Long Mile; but Ogilby's trundle wheel measured the distance as 24 3/4 Statute Miles. Perhaps she meant 'wearisome miles'? Or was she carrying a copy of Ogilby with her, and just assumed his distances were in Long Miles?

Certainly every serious traveller by the 1690s would have been carrying a version of Ogilby – not his huge folio edition but one of the many pirated versions which appeared after his death, in formats suitable for a saddlebag. One I have seen, in the Cambridge University Library, is bound as a softback in beautifully supple leather so that it can be folded or rolled up. New versions continued to appear throughout the next century, with such titles as *Ogilby Improv'd* (1720, the maps redrawn by E Bowen but almost certainly without re-survey) and in 1757 *The Roads through England Delineated*. By this time sufficient turnpikes had been built to make a new survey vital, yet in 1780 we find *The Traveller's Pocket Book* by Ogilby and Potter and in 1785 there appeared *The Pocket Book or Ogilby and Morgan's Book of the Roads*.

Surely Potter and Morgan must have felt obliged to incorporate *some* new material? But that Ogilby's name could still be useful to sell a road-atlas 110 years after his death, and that his achievement is of interest to us even today, is the kind of immortality writers and publishers dream of.

## What did Ogilby omit?

Ogilby's terms of reference were 'to depict the Post Roads for conveying letters to and from London'. The published work covered over 7000 miles of road, and Ogilby reputedly had surveyed three times that amount. What, then, has he omitted which would have been significant?

The rural road network then was probably as extensive as it is today, indeed most of our country lanes were almost certainly in existence but they appear only as side turnings from the post-roads. But some major routes, which we know existed, are missing. Perhaps they were not designated as post-roads.

For Cornwall, Gascoyne's map of 1699 must include all such routes, but they cannot be distinguished from lesser roads. For Devon it is rather more complicated: Morden's small scale map of 1695 shows a little more than Ogilby. Donn in 1765 gives some clues, though some changes must have occurred in the intervening 90 years. We have to avoid assuming that a route important now must already have been important then.

The status of a modern road can be deduced by engineering factors such as how many traffic-lanes it has and how infrequent the junctions are, not to mention a classification system of motorways, A-roads, B-roads, unclassified roads. For 1675 there are precious few clues to relative importance. The post-roads were often no wider than the byways – arguably they were no more than a succession of by-ways strung together to give the appearance of a long-distance route. The main indicator of importance we have is whether a road was used by that tiny number of travellers whose diaries or other records have been preserved.

The most startling omission is the route through Devon and Cornwall we know as the A30. Was it an important road in 1675? On Gascoyne's map its route from Hayle to Bodmin is clearly seen, but how much was it used? The route across Bodmin Moor is discussed on page 8: it was less important than the route north of the moor via Camelford and is probably correctly omitted. From Launceston many up-country travellers returned to Exeter via Oke-hampton. From Launceston to Okehampton there are several possible routes (some truncated by the modern dual carriageway): one goes south of Broad-woodwidger and Roadford (suggestive name) Lake, and across to Bratton Clovelly; another goes past Stowford to Bridestowe. Possibly different routes were favoured at different times, but they may well have co-existed.

The standard route from Okehampton to Exeter was via Crediton, and can still be followed, through Bow: this is to my mind a strange omission. Celia Fiennes, however, reached Okehampton and was forced by flooding to use the route via South Zeal and Crockernwell – actually more direct though she was told it was longer – and her comments are illuminating:

> These rains fully convinced me of the need of so many great stone
> bridges, whose arches are so high that I wondered at it, because the
> waters seemed shallow streams, but they were so swelled by one
> night and day's rain that they came up pretty near the arches, and
> ran in most places with such rapidity and looked so thick and

troubled as if they would clear all before them. This causes great floods, and the lower grounds are overwhelmed for a season after such rains, so that had I not put on and gotten beyond Lanston that day there would have been no moving for me till the floods, which hourly increased, were run off.

Next day I went to Cochen Well 10 miles, mostly good open way except a hill or two which were steep and stony; though this was the longer way and about, yet by reason of the former rains it was the safest, for the lower way was run over by the waters which are land floods from the swelling brooks, which are up in a few hours and are sunk in the same time again – the ways were somewhat dirty.

Thence to Exeter, 10 miles more, but this was the basest way you can go, and made much worse by these rains, but its narrow lanes full of stones and loose ground, clay, and now exceedingly slippery by the rains.

Given the narrowness of the Plymouth-Ashburton road as described by Celia Fiennes, and the obvious problems of taking a vehicle over a virtually trackless Dartmoor, it is unsurprising that when Duke Cosmo III of Tuscany landed with his coach and entourage at Plymouth in 1669, his route to Exeter was via Okehampton. The curious thing is that the road from Plymouth to Oke-hampton avoided Tavistock. It can still be followed most of the way: from Horrabridge take Jordan Lane steadily northward to Moorshop, bear right past Langford to Peter Tavy. Take the bridleway to Mary Tavy and head north across the open moor.

No doubt readers will spot other mysterious omissions for themselves.

## The aims of the present edition

I have included all of Ogilby's maps covering Devon and Cornwall (and part of Somerset) together with his text, and attempted to describe the route his roads take with reference to the Ordnance Survey's Explorer series, which are at 1:25 000. (The numbers allotted to individual maps in the Explorer series have in some cases changed over the years, so please be understanding if I have used a different number from the one on your copy!)

For the rest of Somerset and Dorset, I have included all the relevant Ogilby maps, but for reasons of space have not been able to include his text, nor have I attempted to describe the line he took. Living as I do on the border of Cornwall and Devon, I have attempted to follow many but not all of the Ogilby roads in those counties and have visited some of the problematic points, but with the exception of some border areas did not feel able to do the same in Dorset or Somerset.

When attempting to work out the Ogilby line, I have sometimes been absolutely certain of it, usually fairly confident, and not infrequently downright lost! On several occasions I have been convinced that the surveyors had made a mistake, perhaps after too convivial an evening the night before. Usually, however, further research or reflection has proved me wrong. Their survey was meticulous, though there must be some errors.

There have also been times when I was conscious that more local knowledge, for example of current place names which have not found their way onto the OS maps or street atlases, would have helped. It was quite clear that some points of detail could have been settled by a few years dusting off documents in the County Record Offices. 'Had we but world enough and time...' as a contemporary of Ogilby so marvellously put it.

My purpose has not been academic. I simply wish to share with readers the enormous pleasure which Ogilby and tracking down our ancient road network have given me. Go out there and enjoy it too.

## The material and its presentation

Ogilby's book is massive in format. It consists of 100 numbered plates, each of them a double page spread 15$^1$/$_2$ x 21 inches in size, alternated with a double page spread of continuous text commentary. Each plate contains six or seven strip maps, each reproduced as if it were a scroll. The outer scrolls extend to the full page height. The middle two or three scrolls are curtailed by an ornamental panel in the upper centre of the spread; some of these panels are reproduced in this book as decorations – Ogilby approved of decorations!

The strips were not numbered in the original work, so I have given them letters A, B, etc from left to right. The strip-map reproduced on page 25, which I call '26D', is the fourth strip in Ogilby's plate number 26.

As the outer strips are 13 inches tall, the only way to reproduce them at their original scale in this book has been to divide them in two. I have divided his text commentary strip by strip, and kept the spelling unchanged.

All Ogilby's routes start, where possible, from London, and are measured in miles and furlongs (8 furlongs to a mile), so in his text '138.2' means 138 $^1$/$_4$ miles from the centre of London – the Standard at Cornhill.

One defect of the strip map is the problem of navigating on the return journey! The Ogilby text does actually include instructions for the return, but abbreviated and rather half-hearted. I have omitted them.

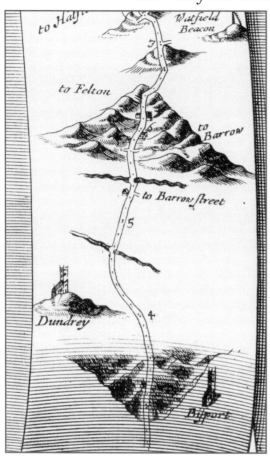

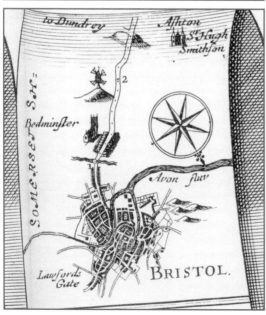

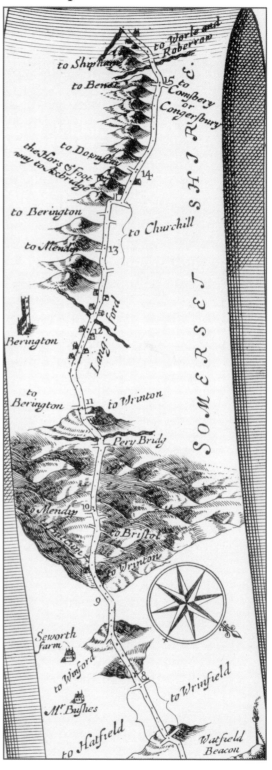

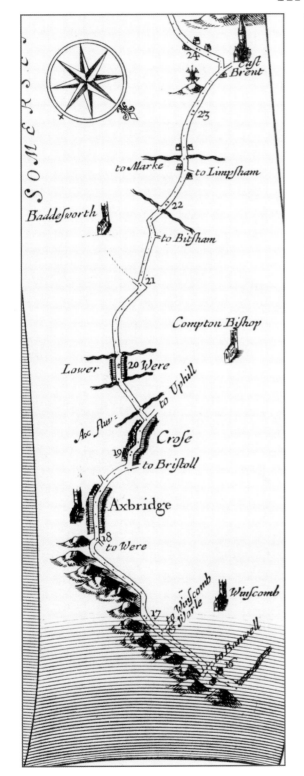

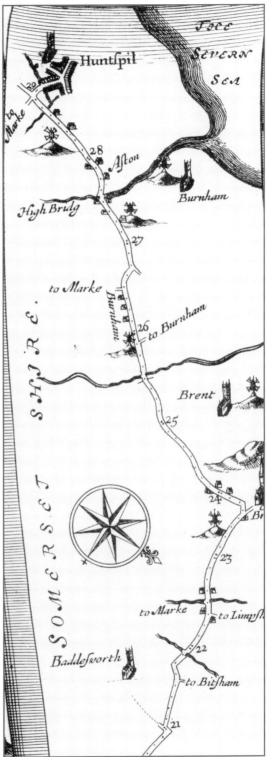

This was a major route or 'Direct Independent' in Ogilby's terms, and he says of it 'The Post Office making this one of their 6 principal roads of England … in general a very good road as any in the kingdom, and as good entertainment.'

It ran through Hammersmith to Staines, Bagshot, Basingstoke, Andover, Salisbury, Shaftesbury, Sherborne, Yeovil ('Evill') and Crewkerne – in other words, what we know as the A30. I have included the section from Burcombe (just south of Wilton, which lay north of the road) to Crewkerne without commentary.

*26C*

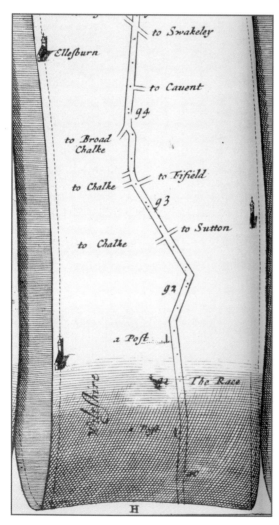
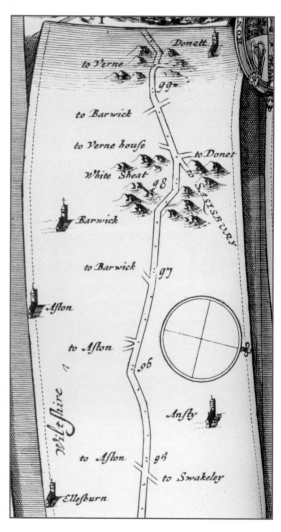

# The Road From LONDON to the LANDS END

### Comencing at the Standard in Cornhill
### and Extending to Senan in Cornwall.

## By IOHN OGILBY Esq.ʳ his Ma.ᵗⁱᵉˢ Cosmographer.

### Containing 302 miles 3 furlongs viz.ᵗ

to Brantfort 10·4 Stanes 8·7 Bagshot 10·0. Hartley-Row 9·0. Basing stoke 10·1 Andover 18·4. SALISBURY 19·4. Shaftesbury 19·4. Sherborn 15·4. Crookhorn 14·6 Axminster 10·2. Honiton 12·4. EXETER 16·4. Chidley 9·4. Ashburton 9·0. Brent 7·6. Plymouth 17·0. Lowe 16·2. Trewardreth 12·0. Tregoney 12·6. Mark....et-Jew 30·2. Pensance 3·0. Senan 10·3.

*26D*

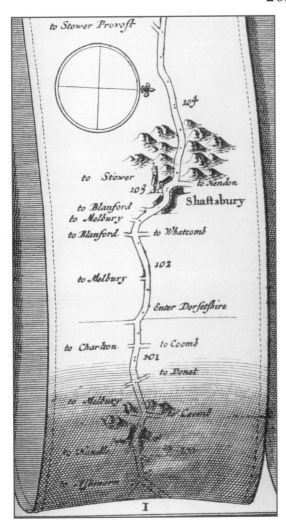

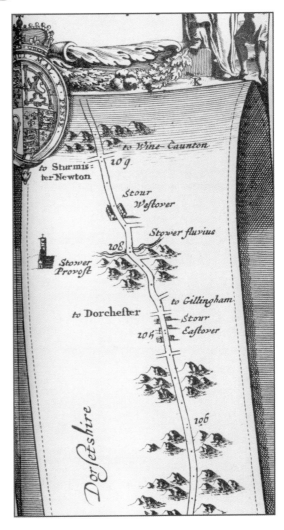

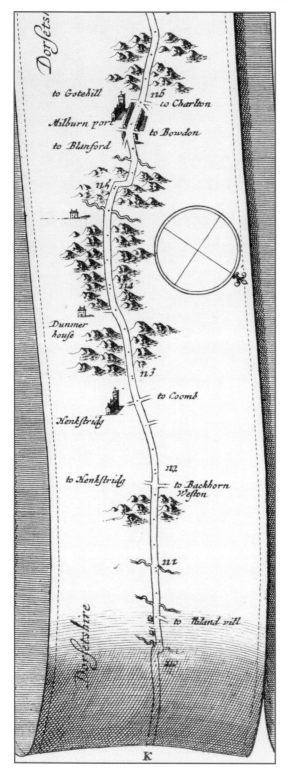

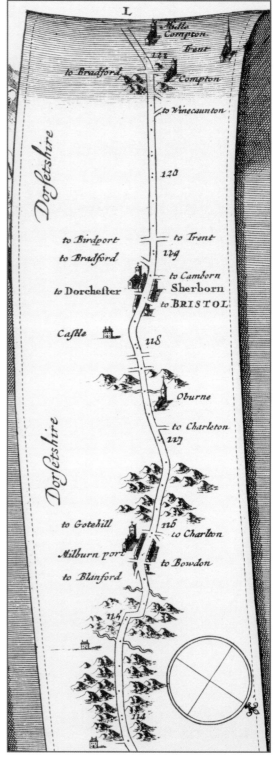

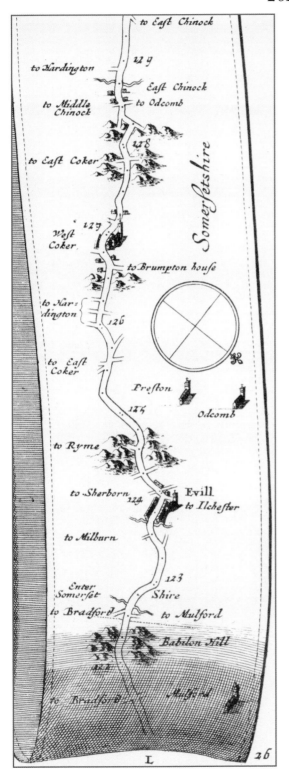

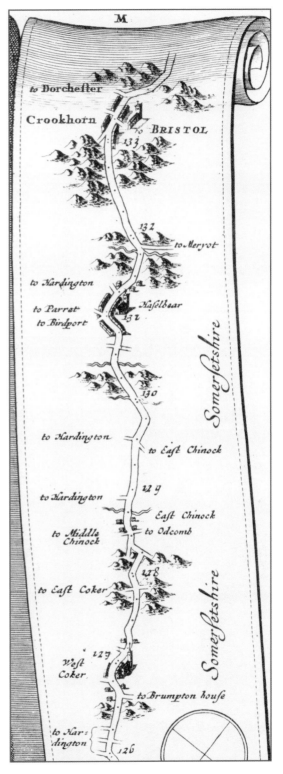

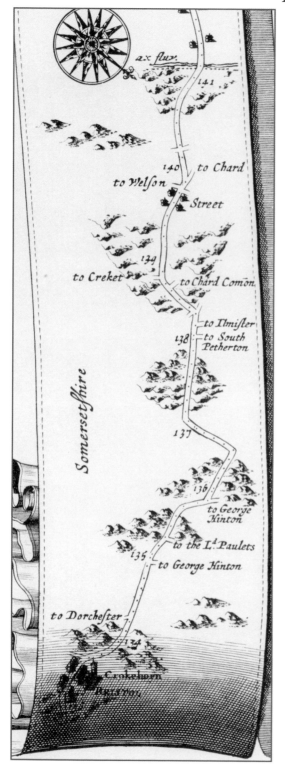

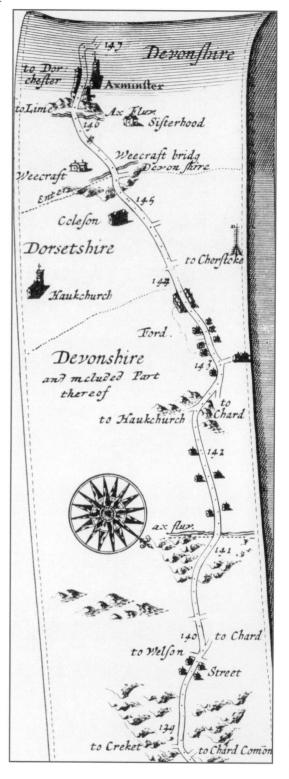

The Continuation of the Road from
LONDON to the LANDS-END.
Plate 3 Comencing at Crookhorn com. Somerset &
Extending to Plimouth com. Devonshire
Containing 82 Miles 4 Furlongs. viz.
From Crookhorn to Axminster 13 Miles 2 Furlongs. to Honiton 9 m. 4 f.
to Rockbere 10. m. to the City of EXETER 6 m. 4 furl. to Chidley 9 m. 4 f.
to Ashburton 9 m. to Brent 7 m. ⅔ 6 furl. and to Plimouth 17. miles.

From Crewkerne Ogilby's route went to Axminster rather than Chard, following first the A30 to Cricket St Thomas, then the line of Fosse Way, B3167. The river marked 'Ax fluv' is not the Ax but a tributary. 'Ford' is now Fordwater. County boundaries have been rationalised since 1675: at that time 'islands' of land belonging to one county could exist within its neighbour.

We brought you to Crookhorn in Plate the Second, at the end whereof you ascend an hill of 4 furlongs, which is seconded with two other ascents; whence crossing a vale you come at 138.2 to a descent of 9 furlongs, at the bottom whereof you pass through a discontinued village called Streat, and leave Chard a market and post-town about a mile distant on the right; then at 140.5 you descend 4 furlongs and enter an included part of Devonshire, where you cross the small river Ax, and pass by several disperst houses and over a small ascent, leaving Esq Titherly's

house on the right, pass through Ford a discontinued village, entering a part of Dorsetshire at 144.2, where you have Hauke church on the left and a beacon on the right.

Hence by Coakson House on the left, you descend a small hill at 145.1 and passing over Weecraft Bridge enter Devonshire, leaving Weecraft House on the left, and Sisterhood on the right, come to Axmister or Axminster at 146.2, a town indifferent large, extending 3 furlongs on the road; is seated on the Ax aforesaid and near the edge of the county towards Somersetshire; it was a town of good account in the time of the Saxons, whose princes slain at the battle of Brunaburgh were here interred. It at present enjoys a good market on Saturdays.

'Beyond Chard to Honiton is a very bad road of stones and sand, over brooks, spring-heads, and barren downs.'

Dr William Stukely, 1724

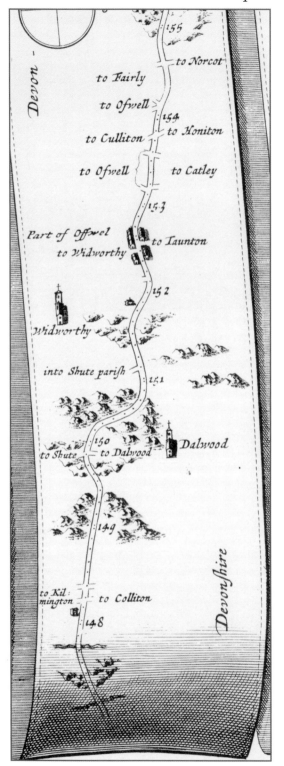

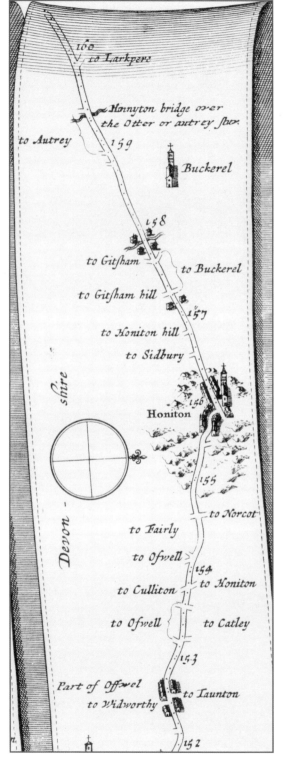

# Axminster - Honiton

Leaving Axminster by the Honiton road, B3261, the route passed on the line of A35 between Kilmington and Coryton Park, ('Collyton'). Then it seems to follow the Roman road (now a 'byway') to Shute Hill Farm and Taunton Cross.

It then seems to follow the minor road to Moorcox Cross before turning left down Wilmington Lane – a sharp descent is correctly indicated! – into 'part of Offwel', which is actually Wilmington. The descent into Honiton from Mount Pleasant was much steeper than the present A35, with its elegant cottage and turnpike gate (separated to allow for today's wide road).

Did Ogilby's route go by way of Tower Farm, or by an even more direct route past Springfield Farm?

From Honiton the line was again the Roman road.

Did the surveyors mishear Feniton Bridge as 'Honnyton Bridge', or was that its name at the time?

Leaving the town you cross the Yare, several hills and small waters or rills, and by Dalwood church on the right and Widworthy on the left, come to part of Offwell, a village of some accommodation.

At 154.6 you descend 7 furlongs and enter Honiton a Borough town of 4 furlongs extent and good entertainment. It enjoys several privileges, as sending burgesses to Parliament, and has a very considerable market for corn, cattle etc on Saturdays.

From Honiton you pass by several disperst houses on the road, and by Buckrel church on the right; then at 159.3 you over Honiton Bridge cross the River Otter or Autre...

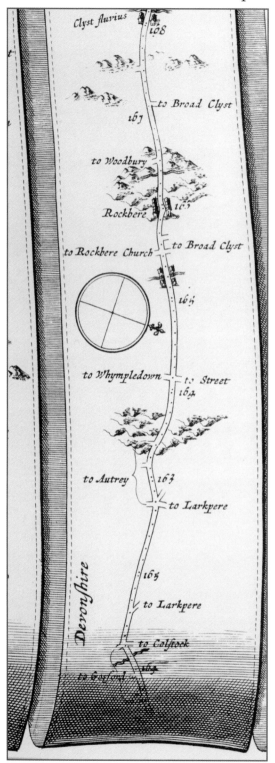

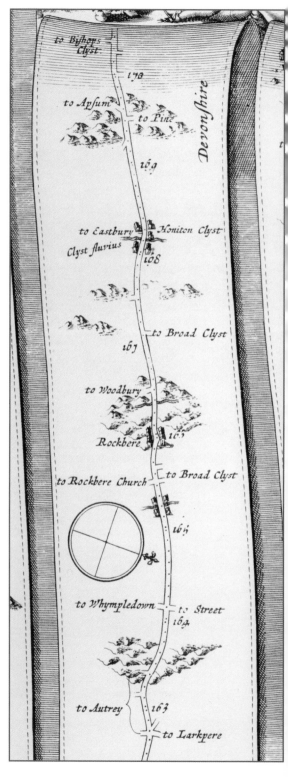

# Fenny Bridges - Exeter

The line of the old A 30 is followed. At the Hand & Pen the directions to 'Street' and 'Whympledown' seem transposed.

…whence an irregular road, descending a hill, conveys you to Rockbere a small village, where you cross a vale and brook, and at 168.1 pass through Honiton-Cliss a little village, at which place you cross the River Clys; then ascending some small hills, and by some disperst houses, come at 172.1 to the City of Exeter, of which take this general account.

Exeter or Excester, a large, well-built, compact and well-inhabited city, called by Ptolemy Isca, by Antonine Isca Damnoniorum; by the Saxons Exan-ceaster and Monketon, *a monachis*; by the Britains, Caer Isk and Pen Caer. It is seated on a small ascent, and on the banks of the River Ex; is about a mile and a half in circumference (excluding its suburbs which are large) containing fifteen parish churches besides its cathedral, which is a curious structure, to which diocese belong the counties of Devon and Cornwall, and hath four arch-deacons, viz of Cornwall, Exeter, Barnstable and Tiverton. The walls of this city were first built by King Athelstone, which gives entrance by five gates; near the East Gate of which stands the ruins of Rugemont Castle, formerly the palace of the West Saxon kings and after of the Duke of Cornwall. This city hath been much harass'd and spoil'd, viz, by the Danes, the Earl of Devonshire, Perkin Warbeck, the Cornish rebels, and the Parliament forces, and its river choked up by the said Earl of Devonshire, that at present they are forced to lade and unlade their goods at Topsham, a place about three miles distant; yet for all this it is in a flourishing condition, drives a good trade, is well frequented by merchants, etc. Is governed by a Mayor, Recorder, 24 Aldermen, etc, sendeth burgesses to Parliament, is dignified by giving title to the Right Honourable John Earl of Exeter, etc, and hath two grand markets weekly on Wednesdays and Fridays, which are well furnished with all sorts of provisions etc.

'From Exeter I went to Honiton, 15 miles, all fine gravel way, the best road I have met with in all the West.

'Thence I went to Axminster, seven miles more, but not so good way, being much in lanes stony and dirty and pretty much up and down hills, like the other parts of those countries.'
Celia Fiennes, 1695

'The road [from Exeter to Axminster] was through an uneven country, divided into fields under the plough, and spacious meadows for feeding cows in which this district abounds. At first we suffered a good deal of incovenience, because they had to travel a road full of water, and muddy though not deep.'
*Travels of Cosmo III*, 1669

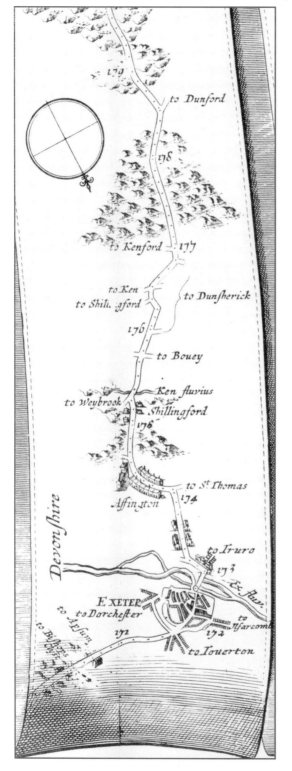

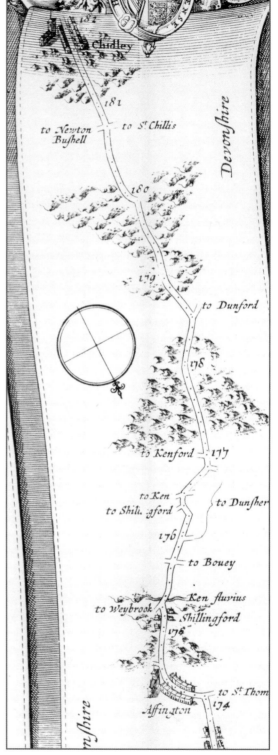

# Exeter - Chudleigh

Exeter was then a more manageable size than it is today. The road 'to Ilfarcombe' is curiously named, as Crediton or Barnstaple might have been expected.

For the Truro route, see 69A.

From Alphington the line at first appears simple – through Shillingford Abbot, Shillingford St George and Clapham, then through the Haldon plantations to what is marked on OS110 as the old Exeter road and into Chudleigh.

But the first 'Shillingford' marked at one mile from Alphington is Shillingford Abbot. There is a turning back on the right to Waybrook Cottages. The water crossed here is not the River Kenn, but Matford Brook. 'To Bouey' must be to Bowhay Farm. There is no sign of Shillingford St George, except as a turning on the left, nor of Clapham. Was there a line north of both, now lost, or did the surveyor's notes get a little muddled?

The turn 'to Dunford' is almost 3 miles from 'Ken fluvius', at the top of Haldon. Probably this was at or near SX885848. The crossroads a mile before Chudleigh is presumably at Milestone Cross, though St Chillis is a mystery. Was Trusham church once dedicated to St Chillien?

The left turn would indeed lead to Newton Bushell, now Newton Abbot, by connecting with the Dartmouth-Newton-Exeter road as it crossed Haldon (see page 107).

Leaving Exeter, you over a fair stone bridge over the foresaid Ex, and at 174.3 pass through Affinton a village of 2 furlongs extent and some accommodation; then ascending and descending you pass through Shillingford a small village, and at 177.1 ascend an hill of 9 furlongs height, and crossing a vale, descend another of the like quantity; whence again you cross a vale, and enter Chidleigh or Chidlay, of 3 furlongs extent and good entertainment; seated on the Teign and enjoys a good market on Saturdays.

'From [Exeter] I passed the bridge across the River Ex to Chedly, which was nine miles, mostly lanes and a continual going uphill and down, some of them pretty steep hills… On these hills, as I have said, one can discern little besides enclosures, hedges and trees; rarely can see houses unless you are descending to them; they are always placed in holes, as it were, and you have a precipice to go down to come at them. The lanes are full of stones and dirt, for the most part because they are so close [enclosed] the sun and wind cannot come at them, so that in many places you travel on causeys which are uneven also for want of repair.'

Celia Fiennes, 1695

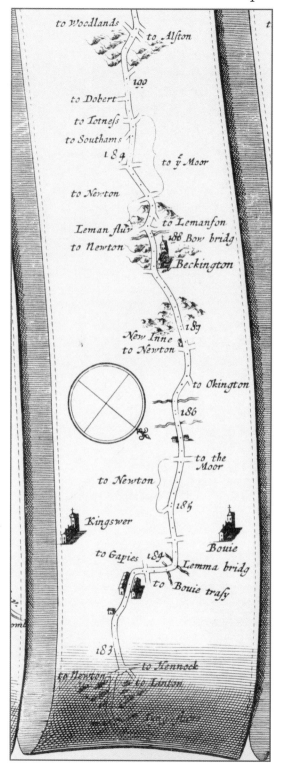

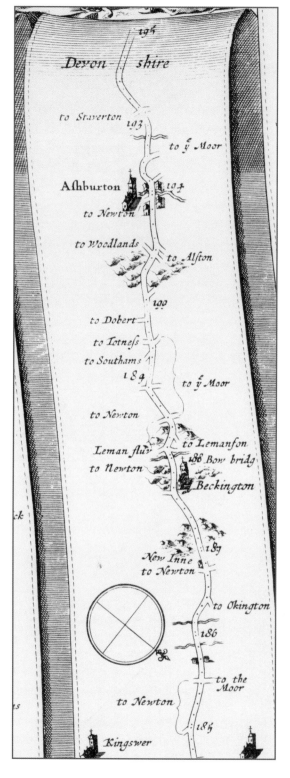

# Chudleigh - Buckfastleigh

Leaving Chudleigh by the main street, there is another turn to Newton (though surely it should come before not after the river crossing to pass through Gappah?), a turn back right to 'Linton' (Lyneham?) and another to Hennock – perhaps the bridleway through Finlake Leisure Park?

Modern developments – clayworks, industrial estates, etc – make the next section inspired guesswork.

Presumably the unnamed village is Chudleigh Knighton. Why the sharp right then left? Maybe this led around the early stages of the clay pit, then across to the bridleway leading to Little Bovey Farm, then past Heathfield Primary School.

Is 'Kingswer' church actually Kingsteignton, over 3 miles away?

It is a relief to reach firmer ground with the New Inn (the 'Welcome Stranger' now stands on the site) just short of Bickington, bearing left up to the church rather than taking the turnpike by-pass.

This is an interesting section to explore on the ground.

The Ogilby route joins A383 just before that in turn joins the modern A38 dual carriageway. Ogilby's route then became the B3352 through Ashburton, past Peartree Cross to a point just before the Dart Bridge.

At the end of the town you cross the Teigne aforesaid, descend a small hill, leave Bovy Tracy church on the right and Knighton on the left, pass by several dispersed houses and New Inn on the left, and ascending a small hill come to Beckington a little village at 187.6 where you cross the Leman and ascend a small hill.

At 190.7 you come to Ashburton an indifferent large Borough town, seated on a branch of the Dart. It is beautified with a fair church, elects parliament men, and hath a well furnished market with corn, cattle etc on Saturdays.

Leaving the town you at 193 miles in a vale cross the Dert [sic] and a mile beyond pass through Buckfastleigh a small village.

---

'From Chedly to Ashburton is 11 miles more, in all 20 miles from Exeter, the roads being much the same as before. This Ashburton is a poor little town – bad was the best inn. It is a market town, and here are a great many dissenters and those of the most considerable persons of the town: there was a presbyterian, an anabaptist, and a quakers' meeting.'

Celia Fiennes, 1695

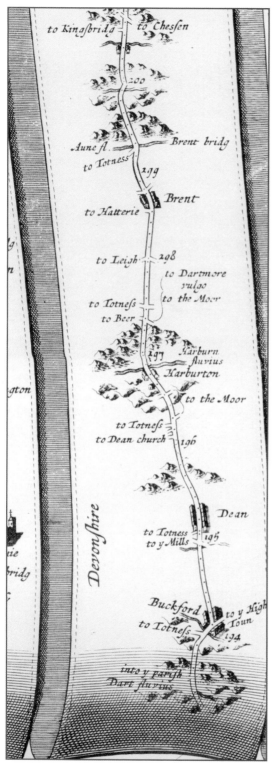

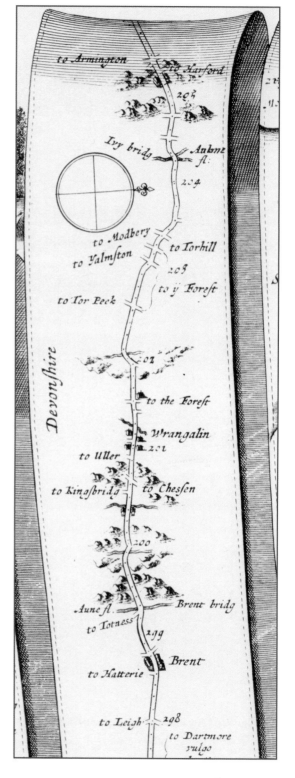

# Buckfastleigh - Ivybridge

At 'Buckford' (Buckfastleigh) the map is easy to follow. The Totnes road probably went via High Beara, Bumpston Cross, Staverton Bridge, Huxham's Cross, Shinner's Bridge, then through Cott and Longcause.

'Dean' is now Upper Dean, where the old road diverges from A38, and then along a track, rejoining the lane to Harbourneford ('Harburton').

After Brent Bridge, Ogilby's route runs north of both the dual carriageway and its predecessor, through Wrangaton, Bittaford (just a stream without a name at 202 miles from London) and along the line of B3213 through Ivybridge.

Hence at 195.1 you come to Dean Prior another small village, and at 196.7 in a vale, cross the small River Harbone, and pass through Harburton a little village.

At 198.6 you proceed through Brent a small market and post-town; and 5 furlongs further over Brent Bridge you cross the small River Aune; whence crossing several hills and waters, you are brought at 201 miles to Wrangatin a little village, and at 203.3 by a cross in the road, come a mile further to Ivy Bridge over the River Aume…

'Thence I went to Plymouth, 24 long miles, and here the roads contract and the lanes are exceeding narrow and so covered up you can see little about; an army might be marching undiscovered by anybody, for when you are on those heights that show a vast country about, you cannot see one road. The ways now become so difficult that one could scarcely pass by each other, even the single horses, and so dirty in many places, and just a track for one horse's feet, and the banks on either side so near, that were they not well secured and mended with stones stuck close like a dry wall everywhere when they discover the banks to break and moulder down, they would be in danger of swallowing up the way quite; for the quicksets and trees that grow on these banks (which are some of them natural rocks and quarries, others mended with such stone or slate stuck edgeways to secure them) loosen the mould and so make it moulder down sometimes. I passed through several little places and over some stone bridges. The waters are pretty broad, so there are four or five arches in most bridges, all stone…

'This country being almost full of stone, the streets and roads too have a natural sort of paving or pitching, though uneven. All their carriages are here on the backs of horses, with sort of hooks like yokes stand up upon each side of a good height, which are the receptacles of their goods, either wood, furze, or lime, or coal, or corn, or hay, or straw, or what else they convey from place to place, and I cannot see how two such horses can pass each other, or indeed how in some places how any horse can pass by each other, and yet these are the roads that are all hereabouts. Some little corners may jut out that one may a little get out of the way of each other, but this is but seldom.'

Celia Fiennes, 1695

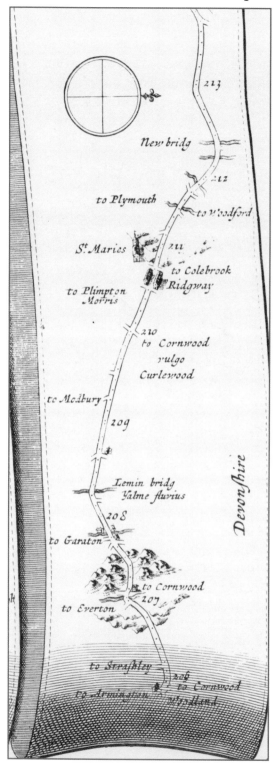

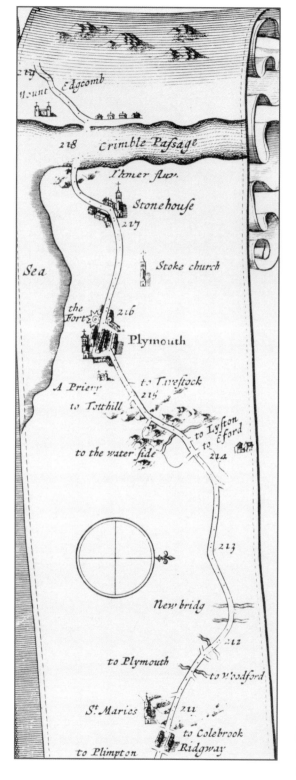

# Ivybridge - Plymouth

After Ivybridge Ogilby's route goes along Woodland Road. (Woodland is a suburb of Ivybridge and Woodland road passes north of the Dame Hannah Rogers School, and heads direct for St Austin's Priory). Did it make a dog-leg up to Cadleigh Cross, or did it go through the industrial estate? Either way it reached 'Lemin Bridge' or 'Lynam Bridge' – Lee Mill as we now know it.

The old road can be seen on the modern map adjacent to the dual carriageway. Once within Plympton it followed the line of the road now called Ridgeway, and the modern Plymouth Road. In Ogilby's time the part of the town which lay on Ridgeway, between George Lane and Station Road, was itself called Ridgeway, as it still was in Donn's 1765 map.

Plympton St Maurice, also known then as Plympton Earl, must still have been the real heart of the town and it may seem surprising that the post-road avoided it – but this happened elsewhere, for example at Fowey, St Austell and Launceston: see page 47.

Crossing the Plym near Marsh Mills roundabout, Ogilby's route followed Old Laira Road through open countryside, past Lipson Vale and presumably down Lipson Road and Exeter Road to the city centre, and along Millbay road to Cremyll Ferry.

…then through Woodland a little village at 205.7, cross a vale at 207 miles, and at 208.2 over Lynam Bridge cross the River Yalme, little else offering itself, till at 210.5 you pass through Ridgway a small village, and leave St Mary's church on the left, where you descend 3 furlongs, and at 212.3 pass over New Bridge, then ascending and descending come to Plymouth at 215.3, a port town of which take this general account.

Plymouth or Plinmouth so called from the River Pline, on which and the Tamer it is situate at their influx into the sea; a place of great strength both by art and nature, which by the occasion of a commodious port and haven, from a poor village has become a fair, large, well-inhabited and well-frequented Borough and Town Corporate, seeming rather a city than a town; tis a place (though containing but 2 parishes) of great importance to the King and Kingdom, where men-of-war and merchants' ships may ride free from the danger of the sea or enemies; the haven is fortified on both sides and defended with a powerful fort, hath on the south side a pier, and in the midst St Nicholas Isle, with a chain to lock over if occasion be, and to the great strengthening of it his present Majesty hath built a fair citadel which is well manned, and hath many pieces of Ordnance mounted thereon.

This town drives a very great trade, is governed by a Mayor, Aldermen, Common Council, etc and sends burgesses to Parliament, hath 2 markets weekly, on Mondays and Thursdays, which are well furnished with all sorts of provisions, live cattle, etc

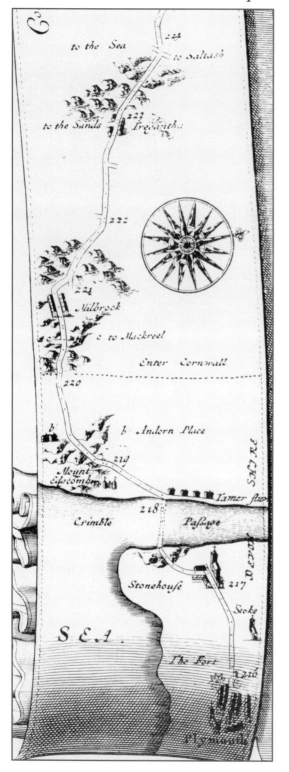

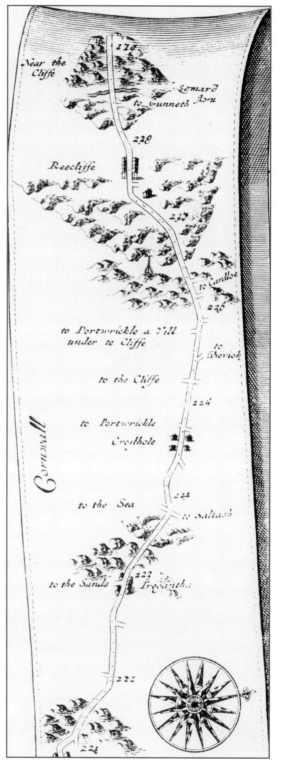

# Millbrook - Seaton

The shoreline at Cremyll is strangely drawn but the route must follow B3247, though diverting along Millbrook Lake, past Tregantle and Crafthole. At Battern Cliffs it followed the coast path.

'Reecliffe' is Downderry, 'Gunneth' is Tregunnick, 'Lemard fluv' is the River Seaton. The comment 'Near the cliffe' suggests a route along the present coast path.

To Plymouth we brought you in Plate the Third, whence you pass by Stoke Dameron to the right, and at 217.1 come to Stonehouse a village of 2 furlongs extent, and 5 furlongs further to Crimble Passage over the Tamer, which is here crossed by a ferry of 4 furlongs; at your landing you leave Mount Edgcomb on the left, and ascending and descending leave Andorn Place on the same hand; then crossing a sand you enter Cornwall at 220.2 where you ascend a small hill, and presently descending again enter Millbrook a village of 2 furlongs extent and some accommodation.

In Millbrook you ascend a hill of 6 furlongs and at 223 miles enter Tregantha a little village, where you ascend an hill of 3 furlongs on which is a beacon on your left, which is seconded with a like descent; then at 224.4 you come to Crofthole a small village, and at 226 miles ascend an hill of 2 furlongs on which is a beacon on your left; then a descent of 9 furlongs brings you to Recliff a small village…

'From Plymouth I went one mile to Cribly Ferry, which is a very hazardous passage by reason of three tides meeting. Had I known the danger before, I should not have been very willing to have gone it, not but this is the constant way all people go, and saved several miles riding. I was at least an hour going over; it was about a mile, but indeed in some places, notwithstanding there were five men rowed and I set my own men to row also, I do believe we made not a step of way for almost a quarter of an hour, but, blessed be God, I came safely over; but those ferry boats are so wet and then the sea and wind are always cold to be upon, that I never fail to catch a cold in a ferry boat, as I did this day, having two more ferries to cross, though not so bad or half so long as this.

Thence to Milbrooke two miles and went all along by the water, and had the full view of the dockyards. Here I entered into Cornwall and so passed over many very steep, stony hills, though here I had some two or three miles of exceeding good way on the downs, and then I came to the steep precipices – great rocky hills. Ever and anon I came down to the sea and rode by its side on the sand, then mounted up again on the hills, which carried me mostly in sight of the South Sea.'

Celia Fiennes, 1695

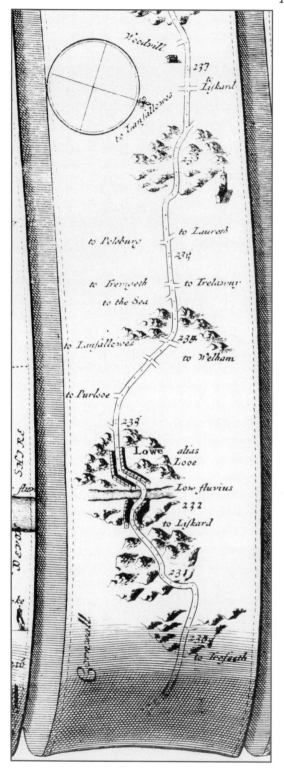

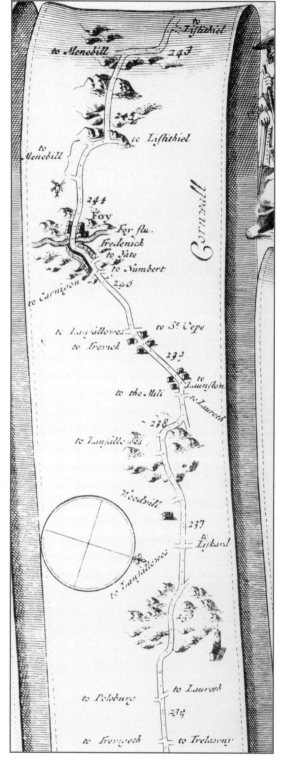

# Looe - Fowey

The route from here into East Looe is confusing. Perhaps it goes via Plaidy, but Gascoyne's map of 1699 shows 'Bodeva' (Bodigga) and may imply crossing the Millendreath valley at SX 269546. Ogilby may suggest a lost path up towards the reservoir (SX 261544) and down Barbican Road.

Looe's medieval bridge, replaced in 1853, was about 100 yards downstream of the modern bridge. After crossing into West Looe, the traveller turned left along the quay, then right up Fore Street towards Portlooe but passing just to the north. Take the B 3359 but go straight ahead at Ashen Cross, leaving Pelynt church to the right. 'Woodvil' is Woodford House, SX 181541, and 'Tredennick' is of course Bodinnick; we pass Hall Farm, not Yeate Farm. Ogilby's men missed Fowey itself and went straight up Passage Lane (Gascoyne's map of 1699 takes the line of A 3082 past Polsco), but Ogilby certainly descends Polmear Hill to Tywardreath church.

….which leaving, you cross 3 repeated vales and in a 4th vale cross the Low over a long stone bridge of many arches, on both sides of which is Lowe alias Looe, divided into East and West Looe; they are commodiously seated by reason of their nearness to the ocean, their chief trade consisting of fishing, they are both towns corporate and send burgesses to Parliament; towards the sea they are fenced with a garretted wall; the town of East Looe enjoys the benefit of a good market on Saturdays; near the mouth of the river is a small island called St George, on which great store of sea-pies breed. Leaving Looe you pass 2 ascents, and by Plinle church on the right, cross 2 vales and leave Woodvil House on the left; then by several dispersed houses you come at 140 miles [*recte* 240] to descend an hill, where you pass through Tredennick, and crossing the River Foy enter the town of Foy alias Foye, which is seated on an ascent. It is strongly fortified, and its haven secured with blockhouses; the town had formerly 60 sail of ships belonging to it, and was renowned for sea-fights; it at present is a good trading place, and enjoys a well-provided market for corn etc on Saturdays.

---

'Here indeed I met with more enclosed ground, and so had more lanes and a deeper clay road, which by the rain the night before had made it very dirty and full of water in many places; in the road there are many holes and sloughs wherever there is clay ground, and when by rains they are filled with water, it is difficult to shun danger. Here my horse was quite down in one of these holes full of water, but by the good hand of God's providence which has always been with me ever a present help in time of need, for giving him a good strap he flounced up again, though he had gotten quite down his head and all, yet did retrieve his feet and got clear off the place with me on his back.'

Celia Fiennes, 1695

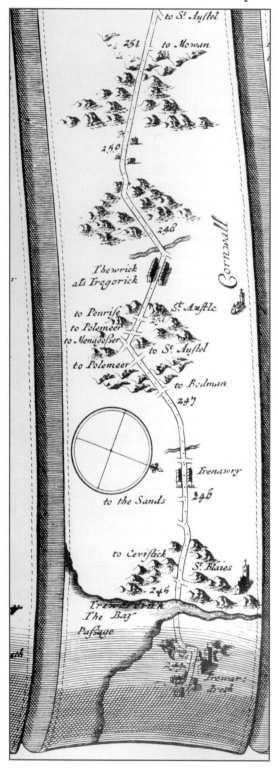

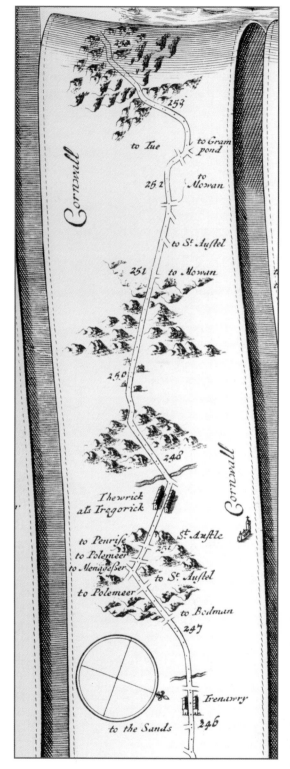

# St Austell

The estuary land had not been drained; there was a river passage by ferry to Par. It is not clear exactly which route was followed: probably Par Lane to St Blazey Gate, but there is an interesting footpath through Biscovey. 'Trenawry' may well be Trenowah (SX 044535).

The next fixed point is Tregorrick, south of St Austell. I am fairly certain that the route involved the footpath leading from a road called Hillside (opposite Tesco), across the railway track and the Charlestown Road, then south of Penrice Community College, curving down to the cross-roads at SX 028514. Then we turn right along Tregorrick Road.

This post-road has already avoided the centres of Plympton and Fowey, and now avoids St Austell, where Celia Fiennes found excellent accommodation. It will later avoid Truro. Another road similarly avoids Launceston, then the chief town in Cornwall. Were they keeping the postboys away from temptations?

The postboys were government messengers and their role must have been to speed long-distance mail rather than to make local deliveries. Letters for the towns would have been dropped at the nearest post-house (an inn where the postboy changed to a fresh horse), to be collected by the recipients.

It is possible that from Tregorrick we take a route through London Apprentice, Little Polgooth and Carnmoggas to Hewas Water, as in 69E, but would we be able to see St Mewan church? The map shows a hill directly across the river from Tregorrick.

I think we must head south of Trewhiddle House, climbing over the golf course, then pass through Polgooth, Sticker and Hewas Water. St Mewan church would, I think, be in view from the top of Trelowth Common, which would have been open pasture. But no right of way or other evidence survives for this route between Tregorrick and Sticker, so I am far from certain about it.

Whence ascending and descending several hills, you come at 244 miles to Trewardreth a small village seated near the sea, and a bay of the same name; thence crossing a ferry you leave St Blais church on the left, whence you ascend and presently descend again. At 246.2 you come to Trenawry a little village, and crossing a vale you pass through Tregorrick a small village and leave St Austell church on the right: then crossing a brook you ascend an hill and pass through Polebooth a scattering village, where you presently ascend and descend, and leave Mowan church on the right; thence bearing to the left you ascend a small hill and cross a vale…

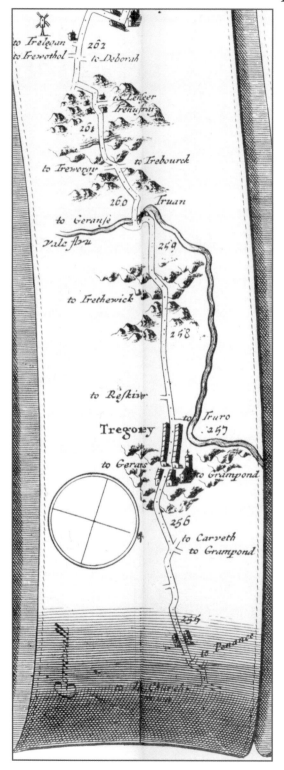

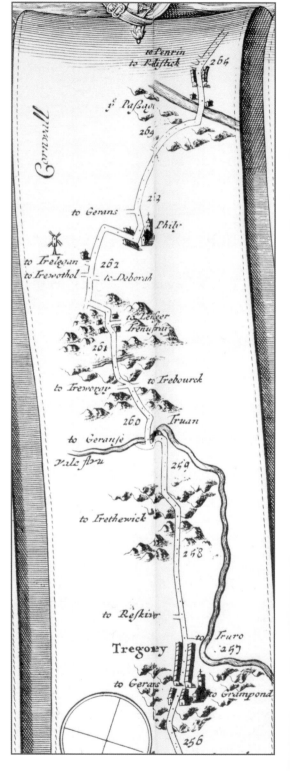

# Tregony - Trelissick

The road to 'Penance' (Penans, SW 954489) presumably diverges at Fair Cross. The buildings by the road may be at Pittsdown Cottage, and Carveth is clear enough. From Tregony Ogilby follows the modern road to Ruan Lanihorne ('Truan') and then the track – as so often, still a right of way – from Trelonk, and through Trenestrall before rejoining the lane to Philleigh, to the King Harry Ferry and across to Trelissick – having avoided Truro completely.

…whence little occurs till at 256.2 you descend an hill, and on it enter Tregny alias Tregony, seated near the sea and on the River Vale, of 5 furlongs extent and good accommodation; was formerly strengthened with a castle, which with the town is much gone to decay, yet as a town corporate sends burgesses to Parliament and enjoys a market on Saturdays.

Hence your road is hilly and sandy, passing through Trevan at 259.3 and Trenustray at 261.2 both small villages; then an irregular way brings you at 262.6 to Philly a small village, and descending an hill you cross Kings High Passage, and 2 furlongs further pass through a little village…

*The route is greatly dependent on ferries, which were simply rowing boats. This print of the Saltash ferry in 1821, 150 years after Ogilby, shows how they coped with the arrival of coaches. Many travellers declared themselves terrified by the crossing!*

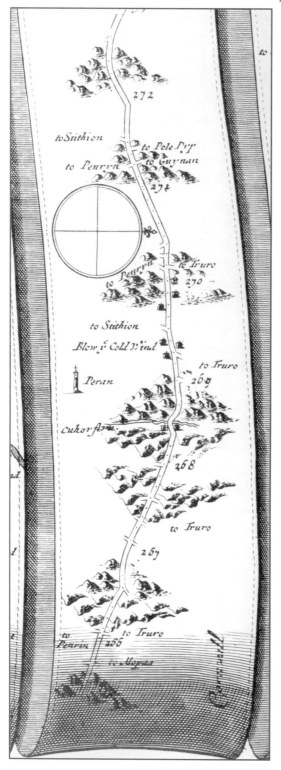

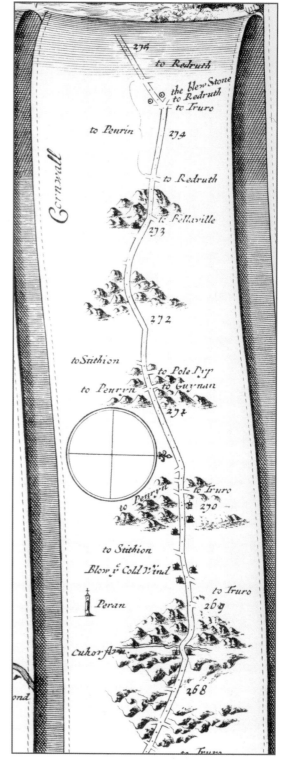

# Carnon Downs - Four Lanes

From Trelissick the route appears to follow B3289 to Carnon Downs, crossing the Carnon River ('Cuhor fluv.) and heading for Coldwind (SW770400). The route more or less followed the present lane past Pulla Cross to Burncoose. 'Bellavill' is Bell Veor in Lanner. We take the lane from Burncoose west past Badger Hill (SW729390) to Ivy House, then a track past West Carvannel Farm to Four Lanes, where the track is called Deep Lane. Within living memory a house on the corner of Deep Lane was called Blue Stone. Was there once an actual stone, or perhaps a pub of that name? I was interested to hear of a local tradition that John Wesley rode down Deep Lane: since it was the main road to Penzance, I think we can be fairly sure that he did!

…thence ascending you pass over a vale, and at 267.3 descend again and cross over another valley, pass through Blow the Cold Wind a little village so called, and leave Peryn church on the left; whence little occurs but passing 5 repeated ascents, and by the Blue Stone on the right…

*Each double page spread in Ogilby's book is surmounted with a cartouche giving details of the road: some are illustrated, as here showing on the left a post-boy with his horn, warning other travellers to make way for him, and the surveyors on the right – with a curious choice of companions*

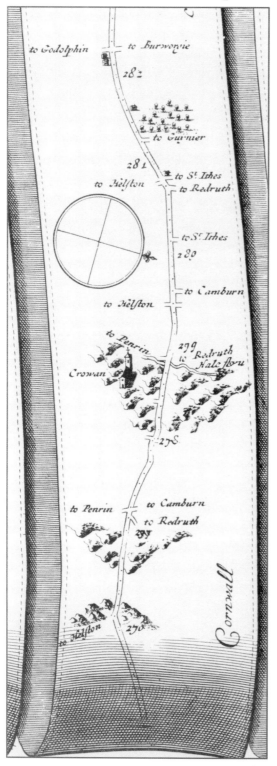

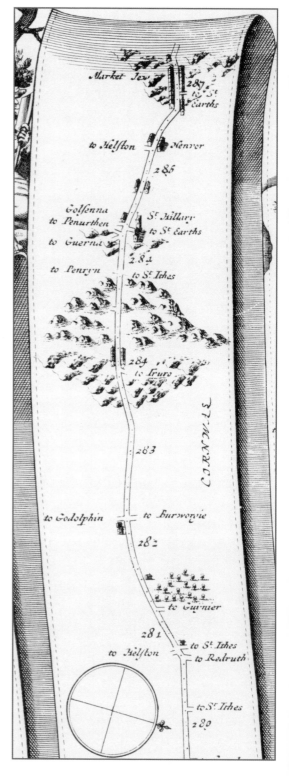

The Continuation of the Road from
## LONDON to the LANDS-END

Plate 4th and last { Comencing at Plimouth com. Devon: & Extending to Senan com. Cornub.

Containing 84. Miles 5. Furlongs, viz.t

From Plimouth to Lowe 16 m. 2 furl to Foye 8'4. to Trewardreth 3'4. to Tregoney 12'6. to Phily 6 m. to Market-Jew 24'2. to Penfance 3 m. to St. Burion 6 m. & to Senan 4'3.

This section starts near Pencoys (SW686382). It followed B3280 to SW671366, then probably took the line of the parish boundary (often a useful indicator of a historic feature) to Carvolth Farm and through Praze-an-Beeble, where a 'public byway' (south of Trethannas) is one of the best-preserved stretches I've found. We now head either for Leedstown, which scarcely existed in 1675, or more probably to the south: note the line across Burnt Downs to Polglase Farm (SW604339). 'Burworgie' is presumaby Bosworgy (SW574331).

We now follow B3280 through Goldsithney and Marazion, the eastern part of which was called Henfor, or by Ogilby Henvor or Henbor.

…till 2 repeated descents brings you by Crowan church on the left. Then passing by some dispersed houses on the road and by a wood on the right, crossing a large vale at 284 miles, where you pass through a small village; a mile beyond you descend an hill and at the bottom pass through a small village, leaving St Hillary church on the right.

At 285.7 you pass through Henbor a small village and 3 furlongs further another little village, entering Market Jew at 286.6 of 4 furlongs extent and good accommodation, seated on an arm of the sea called Mount's Bay, and on a descent; a mean town yet enjoying a market on Thursdays.

'The people here are very ill guides and know very little from home, only to some market town they frequent, but will be very solicitous to know where you go and how far, and from whence you came and where is your abode.'

Celia Fiennes, 1695

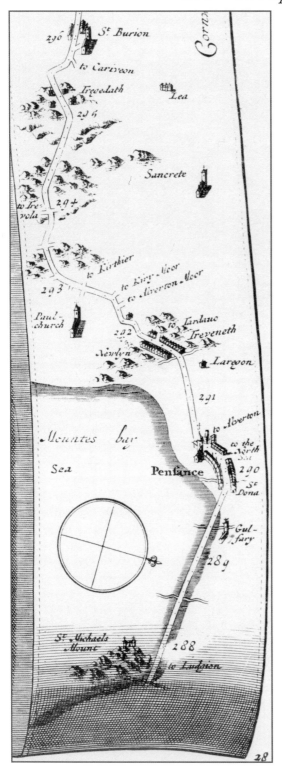

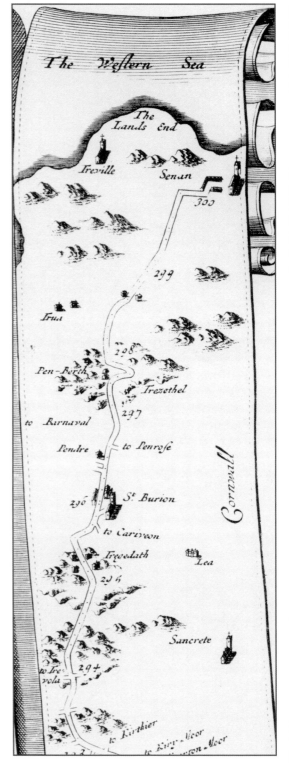

# Penzance - Land's End

From Marazion to Penzance the route seems to be the beach or dunes. From Penzance we go to Newlyn and follow B3315. 'Kerthier' must be Kerris, 'Trevola' is Trevelloe Farm, after which we keep right through 'Tregedath' (Tregadgwith) into St Buryan, leaving by B3283. I suspect we then diverge at Westmoor taking the route down to Tresidder ('Tre-zethal'), Tresidder Bottoms, and Little Trethewey – with Trethewey itself away on the left as 'Trua'; then perhaps by Skewjack Farm and the track leading from SW361252 which would account for the right angle turns.

Was there a church at Trevilley?

Leaving the town you cross a small river, and have St Michael's Mount near you on the left, which is called Hoar Rock, and severed from the mainland by a sandy plain, which at ebb water is passed over on foot. This mount is of a great eminence, the entrance whereof is an open plain, that brings you to a winding and craggy path, which ascending you approach the top on which is a fort or castle, with lodging for the captain and soldiers, and a chapel for devotion; a little distant from the castle is a craggy place called St Michael's Chair, and under the castle is a good road for ships to ride in called Mount's Bay, near unto which is Main Amber Rock, mounted on others of smaller size, so equally counterpoised that it may be stirred, but not moved out of its place.

Hence the Bay accompanies your road on the left to Pensance or Penzans, which you enter at 298.6 [*recte* 289.6] (first passing by Gulfary church on the right) the name signifying an Head of Sands, it extends about 7 furlongs on the road; was almost destroyed by the Spaniards, *anno* 1595, which is since rebuilt, driving a considerable trade, and hath a good market on Thursdays well served with provisions, and fish very plenty.

Leaving the town, you pass by Laregon House on the right, and bearing to the left, pass through Newlin a village seated on a hill, of 4 furlongs extent and good accommodation; whence by St Paul's church on the left you bear to the right, ascend an hill and cross 2 vales, come to St Burien a small village at 296 miles; leave Lea House on the right, Boskena, Trevodran and Pondre houses on the left, cross a vale and pass through Penberth a little village, and by Trua House on the left, are conducted at 300.3 to Senan a village on the utmost promontory or headland called the Land's End in Cornwall, which is washed with the West Sea.

'The houses [in Sennen] are but poor cottages, like barns to look on, much like those in Scotland, but to do my own country the right, the insides of their little cottages are clean and plastered and such as you might comfortably eat and drink in, and for curiosity sake I drank there and I met with very good bottled ale.'

Celia Fiennes, 1695

# The road from London to Barnstable in Devonshire

*... affording in general a good way, especially to Bridgwater, wherein you have near 20 miles of excellent way over Salisbury Plain even from Amesbury to Warminster; but beyond Bridgwater less commendable...*

## 32C

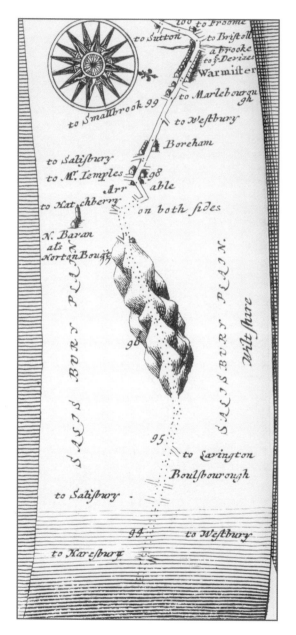

The Road from LONDON to BARSTABLE. in Devonshire.

By JOHN OGILBY Esq.ʳ His Ma.ᵗⁱᵉˢ Cosmograph.ʳ

Containing 193 Miles 5 Furlongs, viz.ᵗ

From y.ᵉ Standard in Cornhill LONDON. to Andover, in the Lands~end Road 66'2. thence to Amesbury 14'3. to Shruton 5'7 to Warmister 13' 0 to Maiden Bradley 6'7. to Bruton 9'3. to Weston~Regis 10'5 to Ascot. 7. 5. and to Bridgwater 9:4.

Thence to Barstable aforesaid, part of Plate y.ᵉ 2.ᵈ 51 4.

Extended from Barstable to Truro in Cornwal 94'5 viz.ᵗ

to Hetherley termiating Plate y.ᵉ Second 21 m.4 furl.

Thence to Truro ✠ in Plate y.ᵉ 3.ᵈ 73'2.

*32D*

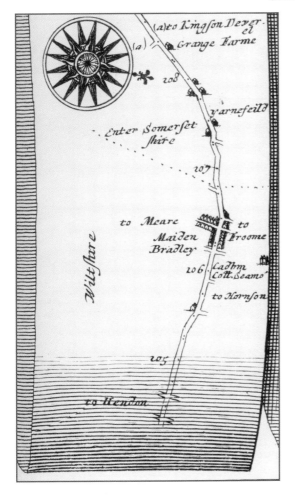

(a) to Kingson Deverel

Grange Farme

108

Yarnefeild

Enter Somerset shire

107

to Meare     to

Maiden     Froome

Bradley

106   Ladhm

Coll. Seams

to Hornson

105

to Hendon

Wiltshire

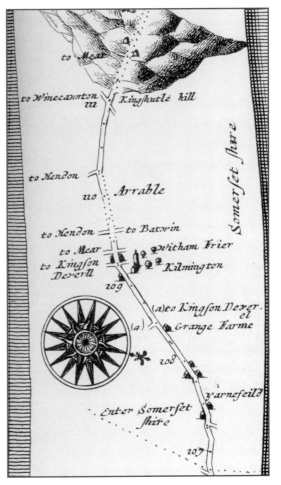

to Mear

to Wincaunton   Kingskutle hill

to Hendon

110   Arrable

to Hendon   to Batwin

to Mear   Witham Frier

to Kingson   Kilmington

Deverll

109

(a) to Kingson Dever.

el   Grange Farme

(a)

108

Yarnefeild

Enter Somerset shire

107

Somerset Shire

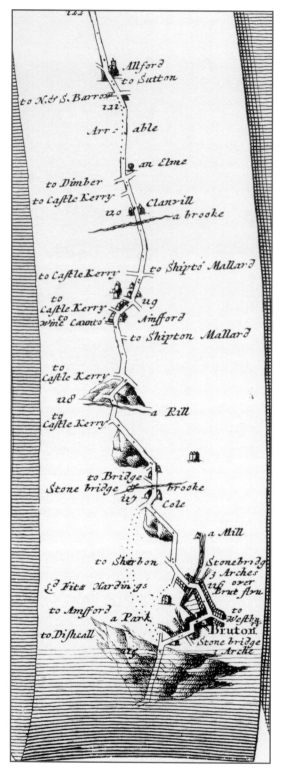

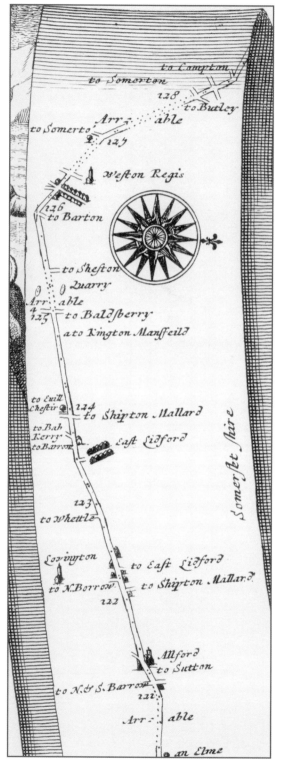

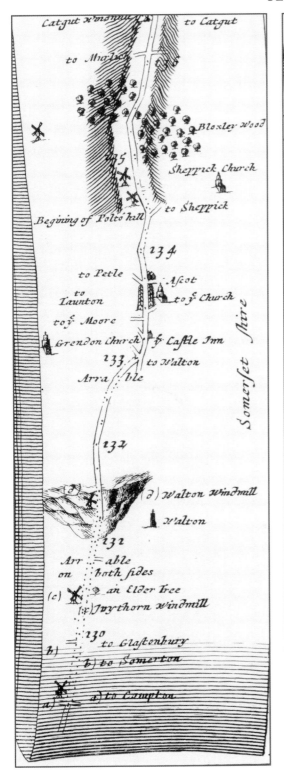

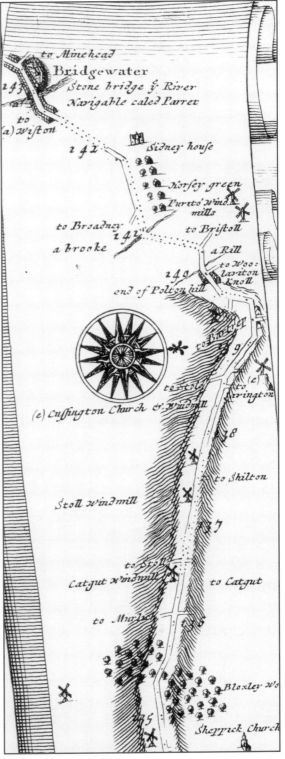

Left strip:

Catgut Windmill · to Catgut
to Market
135
Bloxley Wood
Sheppick Church
to Sheppick
Begining of Polto hill
134
to Petle
to Taunton · Ascot · to ye Church
to ye Moore
Grendon Church · ye Castle Inn
133 · to Walton
Arra ble
Somerset Shire
134
(d) · (d) Walton Windmill
Walton
132
Arr able
on both sides
(c) · an Elder Tree
(c) Ivythorn Windmill
130 · to Glastenbury
(b) · (b) to Somerton
(a) · (a) to Compton

Right strip:

to Minehead
Bridgewater
143 · Stone bridge ye River
Navigable caled Parret
(a) Wiston
142 · Sidney house
Korsey green
Parrto Windmills
to Broadney · to Bristoll
a brooke · 141
a Rill
to Woo=
140 · laviton
Knoll
end of Polton hill
to Baltet
19
(e) · to (e)
to Nrington
(e) Cussington Church & Windmill
18
to Shilton
Stoll windmill · 17
to Stoll
Catgut Windmill · to Catgut
to Market · 16
Bloxley Wo
135
Sheppick Church

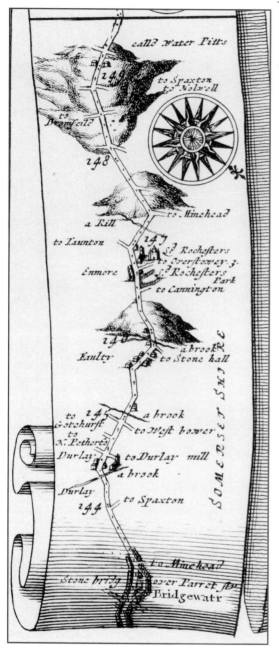

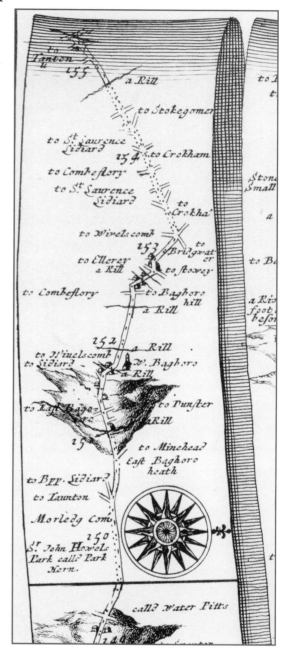

# West from Bridgwater

The London-Barnstaple route is identical with London-Land's End as far as Andover, then from Stonehenge crosses Salisbury Plain to Shrewton, Chitterne, and Warminster.

From there it follows minor roads through Maiden Bradley to Bruton, taking a back route to Castle Cary, then B3153 to Keinton Mandeville.

Then a very straight road runs south of Street to the Polden ridge (alongside today's A39, through several villages) and to Bridgwater. It may seem a bit indirect and wiggly, but having tried the Polden Ridge to Stonehenge section as a route to London on a summer holiday weekend, I can assure you that it's very attractive indeed, and *almost* practical in an absolute emergency as an alternative to the A303.

We join the route at Bridgwater – after which it becomes seriously eccentric! From the town centre we head west to Durleigh – perhaps along the footpath through Brook Farm – and to Enmore. 'Water Pitts' is at ST 207333. We follow the bridleway to Park End and (through the 20 Acre Plantation?) arrive at West Bagborough.

From this point the line is unclear and may in places have been obliterated by changes in land use but in getting there we seem to go well to the north of the direct line through Seven Ash and Coleford Water. It is clear from 33B that we leave Sheet 140 at ST 100344.

In Plate the First we brought you to Bridgwater, a large and well frequented town situate on the navigable River Parret, at whose bridge ships of 100 tun do often ride, 40 sail belonging to the town besides foreigners; it is governed by a Mayor, Recorder, 2 Aldermen, 2 Bailiffs and 24 Common Council men, sends burgesses to Parliament and gives title to the Right Honourable John Earl of Bridgwater, etc, has 2 markets weekly on Thursdays and Saturdays well provided, and 3 fairs annually, viz Thursday sevennight in Lent, Midsummer Day and St Matthew; with a fair church dedicated to St Mary, and several great inns, the Angel, Swan, King's Head, etc.

From Bridgwater at 144.3 you pass through Durlay a small village, and 10 furlongs farther through Faulty a scattering village ascending a hill of 4 furlongs; thence at 146.5 through Enmore, leaving Lord Rochester's house and park on the right; 3 furlongs beyond you ascend again, and at 148.1 descend a hill of 8 furlongs, then over Worledg Common leaving Sir John Howel's park on the left at 150.7 you descend another of 6 furlongs, and pass through West Bagboro a small village, and after passing by several scattering houses on the road, an open way leads you to Willet at 155.3…

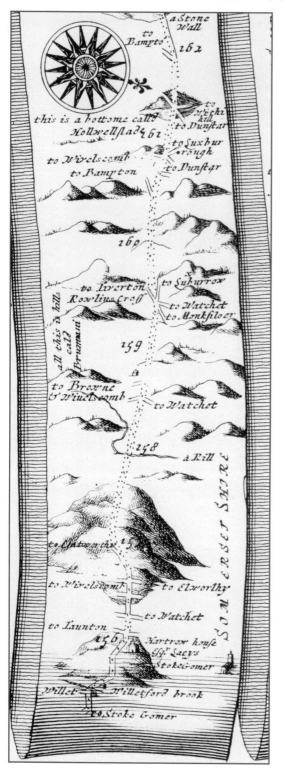

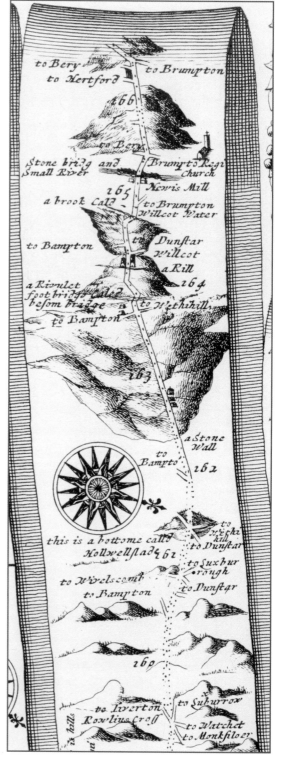

# The Brendon Hills

Starting from ST 100344 the route passes Hartrow Manor and Elworthy Cross before entering unenclosed land (indicated by Ogilby's dotted lines) along the line of B 3224 to Ralegh's Cross.

The present roads are the result of enclosure: the 17th century traveller, on open moorland quite possibly with no single well marked track, would have been anxious not to lose his way, and very relieved to spot the useful landmark of a stone wall, which must have started near Brendon Hill Farm. The turn to 'Wethihill' will be at SS 986323, just before 'besom Bridge'.

Then we pass south of Brompton Regis along Storridge Lane and down Lyddon's Hill.

…there ascending an hill of 4 furlongs, on the which you pass by Hartrow House the seat of Esq. Lacy on the right.

At 156.5 an easy descent brings you to the foot of Brunnam Hill a large ascent of 8 furlongs, your way being generally hilly and open, little occurring else but passing at 159.4 by a small parcel of stones called Rawlin's Cross, and through Holwel-slade a bottom where several roads meet; then at 162.3 leaving the open way, you descend 10 furlongs, ascending and descending several hills and at 164.2 pass through Wilcot a small village; then at 165.2 you pass by Hewis Mill on the right, crossing a small water, and leaving Brumpton Regis church 5 furlongs on the right.

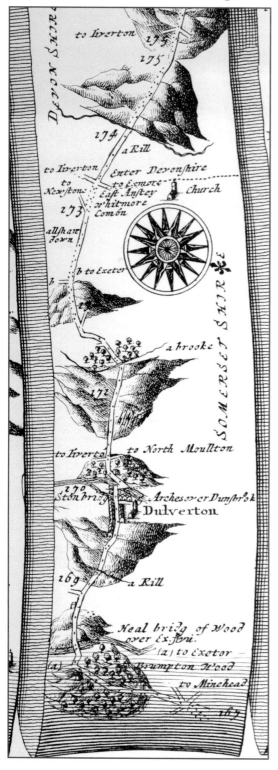

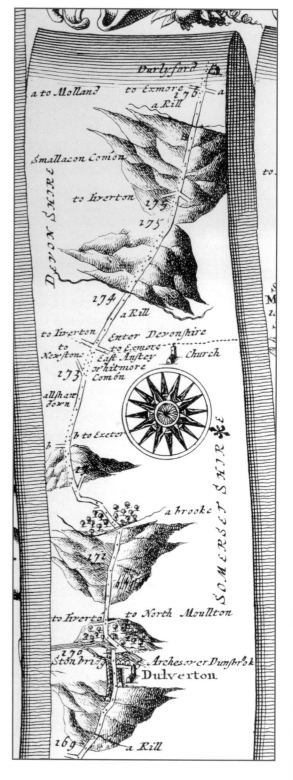

# Dulverton

The crossroads at the beginning of this section is probably at SS 939300: the north-south road is the old Tiverton-Minehead road, see 65F. We descend steeply through the wood, perhaps on the line of the bridleway, to Hele Bridge and enter Dulverton.

After crossing the bridge over the Barle (which Ogilby calls the 'Dunsbrook', i.e. Dane's Brook) we immediately turn right, negotiate a horseshoe bend, then climb a steep hill – a narrow tarmac lane.

We briefly join the newer road, then follow the footpath past Wilway to Streamcombe ('a brooke'), at which point the Ogilby route turns sharply south down the Streamcombe farm track to join the newer road again to Twelve Acre Post and Oldways End.

Oldway Road is the turning 'to Exmore': this is probably a very ancient road, as it heads for what must in pre-Roman times have been a heavily guarded strategic river crossing between Mounsey Castle and Brewer's Castle, both of them Iron Age forts. 'Newstone' is Knowstone.

The B3227 via Bampton is a turnpike dating from 1834. It superseded the Shillingford-Exebridge-Oldways Cross route from Witheridge to South Molton, and at the same time improved the Bampton to South Molton route, which formerly crossed Oakford Bridge.

At 168.3 you cross Heal Bridge of wood over the River Ex; and at 169.4 enter Dulverton seated on the Dunsbrook, a branch of the River Ex, over which is a stone bridge of 5 arches; hath a small market on Saturdays, and 2 fairs annually, Simon and Jude and St Peters, the chiefest commodities then sold are oxen and sheep; it contains about 150 houses, and hath several inns of accommodation.

At the end of Dulverton you cross the Dunsbrook aforesaid, whence an indirect way up and down hills over Alshare Down and Whitmore Common, and passing several small waters or rills, brings you at 173.2 to enter Devonshire, then over Smallacon Common...

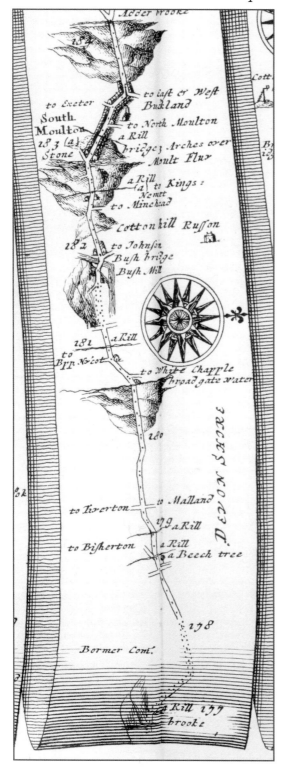

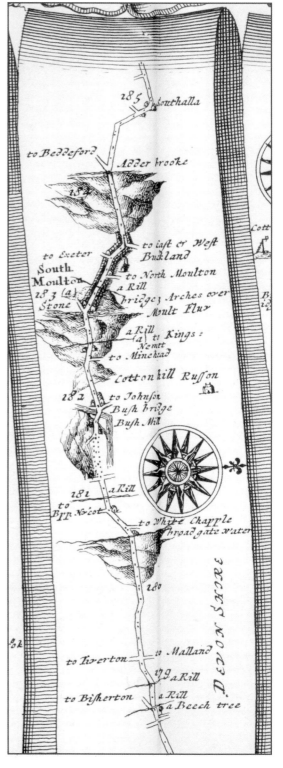

# South Molton

We begin somewhere near Cuckoo Farm (SS 850257). 'Bormer Com.' must be at Bommertown Cross, and we join B 3227 heading with total confidence for South Molton. But our seventeenth century traveller was less certain – looking around for a lone beech tree to confirm he was on the right track! Let's hope it was a massive copper beech.

I conjecture that the beech was at Little Kerscott (SS 789256) and that the fork to 'Bisherton' (Bishop's Nympton) was Port Lane, whilst our route ran direct to Combsland (Old) Cross. I had hoped to find a descendant of the beech at Little Kerscott but looked in vain, though two abandoned tracks are easily inspected either side of a convenient layby.

'White Chapple' is now a hotel, 'Bush Mill' has become Bish Mill and 'Russon' is Rawstone.

South Molton was even in 1675 nearly a mile in length. We leave by B 3227 as far as Kingsland Barton, where we fork right from the road to Bideford (via Umberleigh) and pass Hill Farm and North Hill (which Ogilby calls 'Southalla'). A track now lost appears to have run from North Hill to South Aller.

…Durliford Water, Bormer Common, Broadgate Water, etc by Bush Mill on the right and over Bush Bridge you are conveyed at 182.6 to a stone bridge of 3 arches over Moul fluv. (which rising on Exmore, and 4 miles below this place receiving the Bray, falls into the Taw near Buriton) and enter South Moulton, a Town Corporate governed by a Mayor, Recorder and 3 Capital Burgesses; the Mayor is a Justice of the Peace for one year after his mayoralty, and the eldest burgess likewise; they have a well frequented market on Saturdays, and 2 fairs yearly, viz Saturday before St Barnaby and Saturday before St Bartholomew, at which time all sorts of cattle and other commodities are there sold; their chief trade is in making white serges and felts, having several good inns.

At the end of South Moulton you descend a hill of 4 furlongs, and crossing Adder Brook you leave the acute way on the left that leads to Bediford, and 5 furlongs further pass through Southalla a small village;

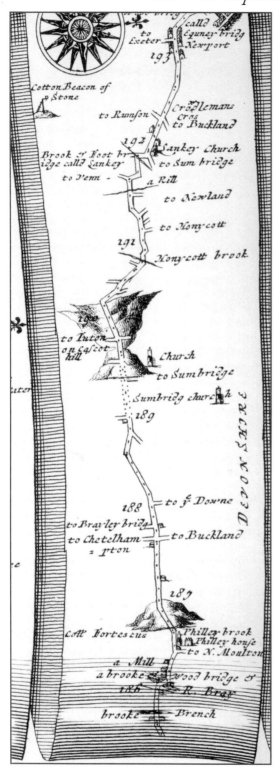

# Filleigh - Barnstaple

We cross Filleigh Bridge. Ogilby's map shows that we pass just south of Filleigh church, but then veer left. The modern road veers right. Why? The bizarre answer is that the church was moved when the mansion was built! Ugly things like roads and churches had to give way to the grand designs of William Kent's landscaping. I think Ogilby's route took the line fossilised on the map, through Lock's Plantation and East Heddon Farm, then up the 'road-with-public-access' at Yollacombe Plantation.

The small settlement at 189 miles may be Kerscott. We pass south of Swimbridge, past Hannaton Cross, Hannaford and Hunnacott Bridge, turn right at Venn Lane End, cross Landkey Bridge, and enter Barnstaple through Newport.

...then at 185.6 you cross Brench Brook, and 3 furlongs further the Bray over a wooden bridge, and at 186.4 by Philley church and Colonel Fortescu's house on the right; whence an indirect way something hilly brings you at 192 miles to Lankey a small village; then at 193 miles you enter Newport of 2 furlongs extent, a good thoroughfare and has a well paved causeway; 2 furlongs further entering Barstable alias Barnstaple, seated on the Taw, a large Town Corporate; sends burgesses to Parliament; is governed by a Mayor, Recorder, 12 Aldermen and 12 burgesses; hath 3 petty markets weekly, viz Tuesdays, Thursdays and Saturdays, and one grand market on Fridays, where are sold all sorts of live cattle and other commodities, and one fair annually.

---

The following diary notes date from 1796 so more than a century after Ogilby. They take the route in the reverse direction.

'Pass through Newport, a large village... the roads in a shameful state: evidently injured by the hedges. Why is not the law enforced? In this country, where woodlands abound and where coals may be had at a reasonable rate, no serious evil could arise were all the hedges in it shorn to their mounds....

Meet a pair of wheels: the first from Bideford. A sweet country but most difficult to be seen! Black limestone road, tolerably good [which brings him to 'Filleigh, Lord Fortescue's noble place' and a quarry].

Pass a string of two-horse carts, guided with reins, in the Cleveland manner...But perhaps his lordship's lime work is the principal cause of the vile roads again, and in the neighbourhood of a great man's residence! The colour of the materials, and the state in which they at present lie, give them every appearance of roads to coal pits. Mount a rich turned swell and enter the town of South Molton.'

William Marshall, 1796

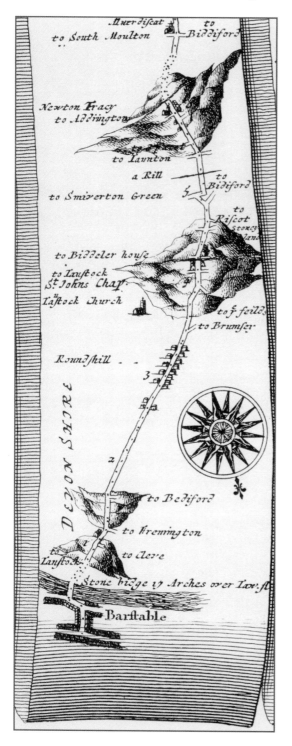

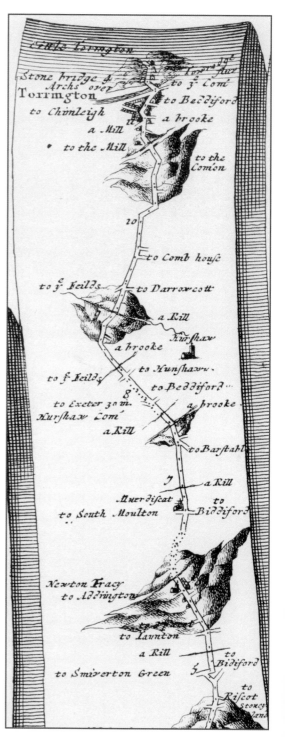

# Barnstaple - Great Torrington

Ogilby starts a new route here, from Barnstaple to Truro. We cross the ancient 'Long Bridge' and keep to the left of the Fremington road, up Old Sticklepath Road, past the church and the crematorium. The line of the road is clear on the map, though there is now no access to the Roundswell roundabout.

Whilst we clearly follow B3232 to St John's Chapel and Newton Tracey, some of the details are puzzling.

St John's Chapel is approximately three miles from the centre of Barnstaple by this route, but Ogilby gives it as four miles. And what is the substantial settlement he calls 'Roundshill' apparently at three miles from Barnstaple, unless Roundswell, just two miles from the centre of the town?

After St John's Chapel, the complex junction must be Prospect Corner, just beyond 'Riscot' (Rushcott). At Alverdiscott we go straight on to Haddacott Cross (joining what looks like the line of an abandoned road from Fremington through Brookham, Higher Lovacott and Stony Cross) then by way of Darracott Cross and a right turn at Coombe Cross we enter Torrington by way of Brent Bridge (SS497197) and leave down the long hill to Taddiport Bridge; we ignore the modern B3227 and go straight ahead, due south up the hill.

From Barnstable you cross a fair bridge of 17 arches over the River Taw, and at 3 miles pass through Roundshill a scattering village; and at 4.2 in a valley through St John's Chapel a small village; and at 6 miles in another valley through Newton Tracy, and 5 furlongs further by Alverdiscot church on the left; from whence a very stony way and over several hills, conveys you at 11 miles to Torrington or Torrington Magna, seated on the Towridg, a large but poor town; is governed by a Mayor, 8 Aldermen and 16 burgesses; its chief trade is making of stuffs; hath a good market on Saturdays for flesh, corn, etc and 3 fairs annually, viz St George's Day, Midsomer Day, and Michaelmas Day; gives title of Earl to his grace Christopher Duke of Albemarle, etc.

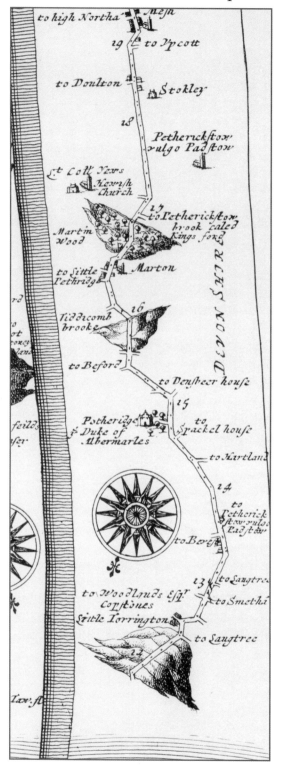

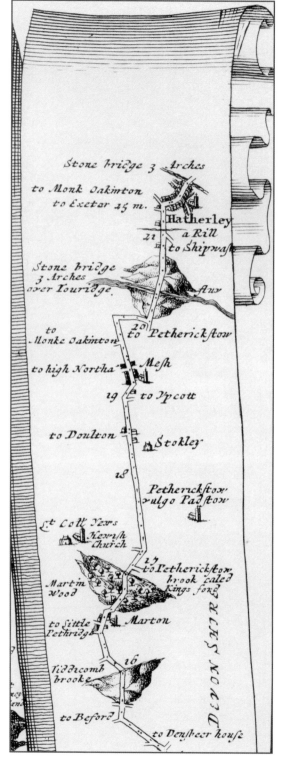

# Taddiport - Hatherleigh

From Taddiport we head due south to Church Ford and into Little Torrington, whence we follow A386. 'Petherickstowe *vulgo* Padstow' is not the Cornish port, but Petrockstow; 'Spackel' is Speccott.

Great Potheridge was the home of General Monck, later first Duke of Albemarle, who engineered the Restoration of Charles II in 1660.

From Chapel Cross (SS 520137) we head south to enter Merton by way of Limer's Lane ('Tiddicomb brook' is now Tythecombelake – 'lake' being a Devon dialect word for a stream or river) and then rejoin A386 through Meeth ('Mesh') into the centre of Hatherleigh, ending at the roundabout on the by-pass.

Leaving Torrington you cross the Towridge over a stone bridge of 4 arches, and ascending pass through Little Torrington, and at 12.4 by another part of Little Torrington on the left; whence at 14.6 you pass by Potheridg a noble structure of the Duke of Albemarle's on the left; and at 16.5 through Marton a small village; descending a hill you cross over Kingsford Brook, leaving Hewish church and Lieutenant-Colonel Yew's house 4 furlongs on the left; then at 18.3 pass by Stokeley House on the right, and 5 furlongs further through Mesh another small village; thence at 20.3 in a valley you over a stone bridge of 3 arches cross the Towridg and 7 furlongs further enter Hatherly alias Hetherley, seated on a branch of the foresaid Towridg, a small town containing about 100 houses, hath a market on Fridays, and one good inn of accommodation, the George.

---

As in the entry for 33E, this dates from 1796 and is in reverse direction.

'Hatherleigh is a mean market town, mostly or wholly built with red earth and thatch. Some of the houses whitewashed, others rough-cast. Four oxen, two horses, two men and a boy, at plough!

A bad turnpike road traces a high ridge of cold white clay, commanding a strongly featured country. Ascend Padstow Hill… Passed the first cart [since Launceston?], drawn in the Cleveland manner! three horses, one in the shafts, the other two abreast, and guided by reins, loaded with bark, for the port of Bideford, to be there shipped for Ireland. Cross a well timbered hollow. Much valuable ship timber in this district. Close woody lanes – how tantalising to a traveller!… Meet a string of lime horses from Bideford, eight or ten miles. Lime here a prevailing manure.

The town of Torrington… is a large inland town, but has no thoroughfare [passing trade] to support it. There is no posting inn in the place! and only one chaise kept for hire. Nevertheless the town is neat and the people alive.'

William Marshall, 1796

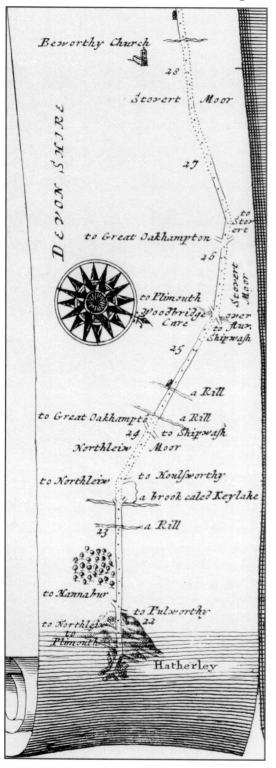

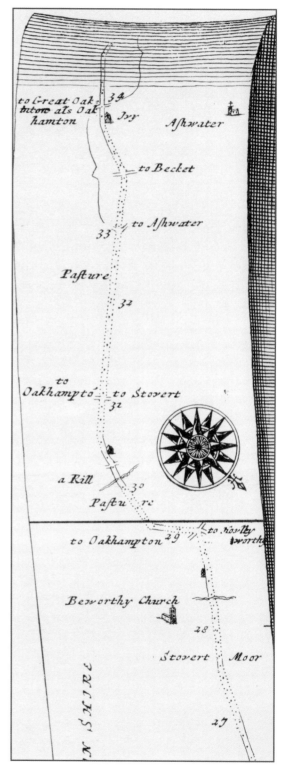

# Hatherleigh - Virginstow

This section is a classic example of a fossilised old road in a landscape which has greatly altered, from open grazing to enclosed farmland.

Starting on A3072 we diverge at Lewmoor plantation (SS515034). Tracks and field boundaries, and then a stretch of road seemingly going nowhere, make the route clear, to Birchen and then as far as Halwill Junction, with a short gap between Wagaford Bridge and Leasefield Farm – though even there the enclosure wall at SS480014 probably represents the southern boundary of the old road.

Halwill Junction is at 29 miles. We turn left along A3079, then right at Henderbarrow Corner to Upcott Cross and south-west past several barrows: barrows can be an indicator of a very ancient trackway, being useful landmarks on the hilltops of an otherwise featureless landscape. The section ends just before Dubbs Cross.

Ogilby describes the section as 'an indirect way' whilst on the map it looks relatively straight. Here and elsewhere I think he uses the word in an obsolete sense, 'undirected', lacking in guidance for the traveller.

In Plate the Second we brought you to Hatherley, whence over a stone bridge of 3 arches you cross a branch of the Towridg, and omitting the acute way on the left to Plymouth, ascend a small hill and pass by a wood on the left; whence you have an indirect way for the most part open, over Northliew Moor, Stovert Moor, etc, crossing the small River Care at 25.3; then at 28 miles by Beworthy church 3 furlongs on the left you come to Ivy at 33.6 a small village on the right…

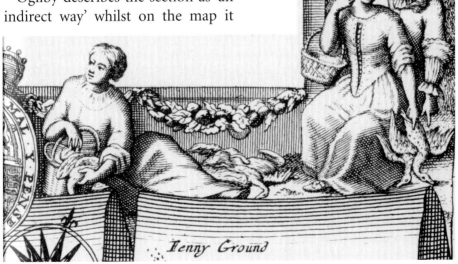

Fenny Ground

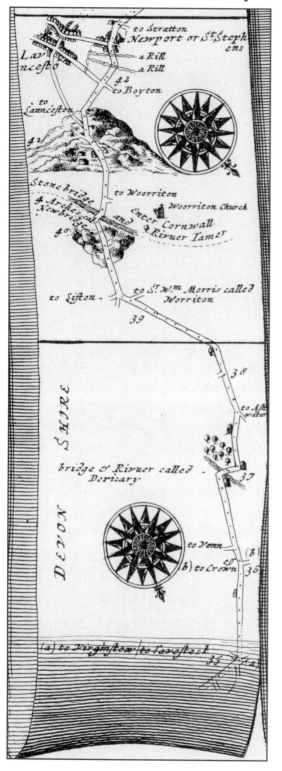

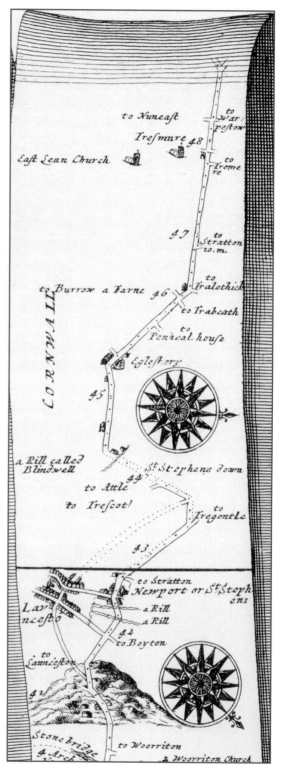

# Launceston

We start at Dubb's Cross (SX 389929) and head south-west to Tower Hill, and cross the River Carey. The junction 'to Ashwater' presumably represents today's A388 at St Giles-on-the-Heath. We cross the Tamar by New Bridge, which is late fifteenth century. The post road avoided Launceston itself, favouring the older settlement of St Stephens. This is strange as Launceston was the administrative centre of Cornwall at that time. Footpaths running south from Homeleigh presumably represent Ogilby's route to the town centre.

From Dutson a footpath cuts a corner to a lane which leads to St Stephen's church, where we cross directly over St Stephens Hill (along Underhayes Lane) then keep right to join the Egloskerry road.

'Tregentle' is Cargentle, a substantial farm beyond Langore.

In the days before enclosure, Ogilby's road probably curved south of the ridge, from Atway Farm, past Glebe Farm and Athill Farm, a curve which can still be seen in the field boundaries and in a stretch of lane and track. It is best seen on sheet OL109. (I live in this area, so inevitably it is on the border of four OS sheets!)

A curious double hedge running east-west just above the tumulus at SX 291859 perhaps represents the line allotted at enclosure, but the farm Twinaways (at SX 300863 but not named on the OS map) may be an indicator that at some stage in the past a traveller could choose which route to take over the moorland.

From Egloskerry the line is little changed. At Tresmeer we continue to head west.

…and at 37 miles cross Dericary a small brook; then at 39.5 you descend 4 furlongs, at the bottom of which over a stone bridge of 4 arches you cross the River Tamer and enter the County of Cornwal, leaving Werington *vulgo* Worriton church and Sir William Morice's house on the right 4 furlongs.

At 40.5 you ascend a hill of 6 furlongs and at 42.0 pass through Newport alias St Stephens, an ancient Borough town, electing Parliament men, and hath 2 fairs yearly, May Day and St Margaret's; near adjoining which on the left is Launston alias Launceston, a large town formerly strengthened by a castle now ruinous. It enjoys several immunities, as sending burgesses to Parliament, and being the place where the County Goal [sic] and Assizes are kept etc; and is governed by a Mayor, Recorder and 8 Aldermen; has a good market on Saturdays, and 3 fairs annually, Whitsun Monday, Midsomer Day and St Leonards.

From Newport an indirect way by several scattering houses on the road brings you at 45.3 to Egleskerry a small village, then by Tresmere church on the left…

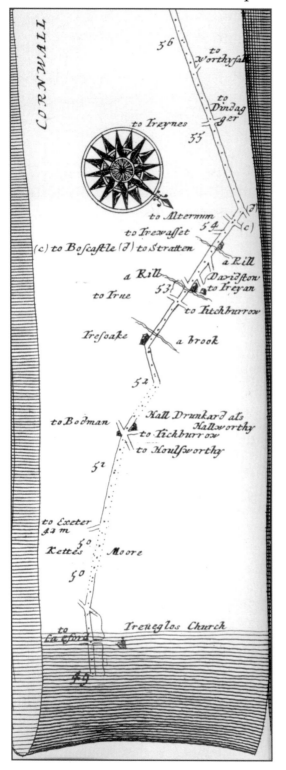

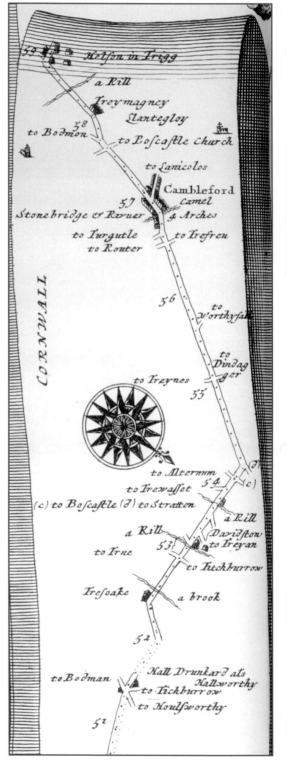

# Camelford

At SX 198869 the old highway we are following from Egloskerry joins A 395, which was in 1675 a lesser road. The hedges at this junction show its old layout: once built, a Cornish hedge stays put for centuries!

'Hall Drunkard' according to OJ Padel was separate from Hallworthy, and a corruption of the Cornish *hal troen-goes*, 'marsh of a promontory wood', which sounds highly improbable to me, as do a great many place-name derivations. I prefer Ogilby's explanation that it was a particularly popular pub!

The turning 'to Bodman' is interesting; this is the lane through Trewinnow, but has left no trace beyond that. Bodmin Moor was avoided by all sensible strangers until the turnpike was built, starting in 1769. In 1754 the proprietor of the White Hart in Bodmin advertised that he had 'at his own expense erected milestones for 22 miles across the large moors that lay between Bodmin and Launceston, the road over which was so difficult before that those not acquainted with it chose to take a circuit of 33 miles, to pass from one town to the other, tho' the way over the moors is no more than 24 miles.'

In fact the milestones had been erected 12 years earlier, and it made little difference. What's an extra seven miles compared to being lost overnight on a boggy, foggy moor? It was not till November 1782 that coaches ran on the line of the A30 – and if you want to experience the road they took, take the turning from the westbound A30 which goes through Temple. Apart from a spot of tarmac, the turnpike road is much as it was.

To return to Ogilby: the post road took the northern route.

'Treyan' is Tregeen, 'Titchburrow' is at SX 147881. We join the A39 at junction (d) to Stratton and turn left, with readily identifiable roads to 'Dindager' – the surveyors relied on someone with a strong local accent! – and Worthyvale, an estate at Slaughter Bridge. After Camelford, this section continues to Helstone.

…then by Tresmere church on the left and Treneglos on the right, and over Kettes Moor; at 51.4 you come to Hall-Drunkard alias Halworthy, a noted inn affording as good entertainment as any on the road; then at 52.4 you pass by Tresoak on the left, and at 53.2 by Davidstow on the right, both small villages; from whence little occurs till at 56.6 you enter Cambleford, seated on the Camel, a small town scarce numbering 50 houses, is in the parish of Lanicolas a mile distant, yet sends burgesses to Parliament, and is governed by a Mayor, Recorder and 8 Magistrates; has a small market on Fridays and 3 fairs yearly, the 15th of May, the 7th of July and St John's in August, having some inns affording good accommodation. At 58.1 you pass Tremagny on the right, and at 59 miles through Helson in Trig a small village…

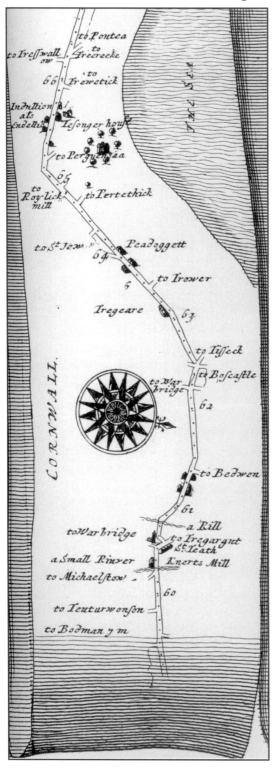

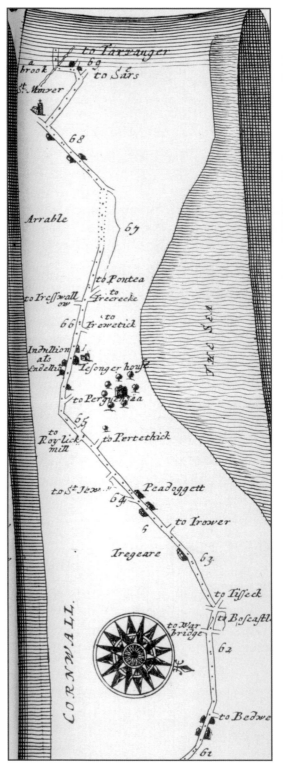

# St Teath - Rock, avoiding Wadebridge

We follow A39 to Knightsmill, but keep right into St Teath – the Allen valley A39 road is a later addition.

The left turn to 'Warbridge' is worth investigating on the ground, through Trewethen and Trelill to St Kew Highway and on towards Wadebridge with its magnificent medieval bridge. This, rather than Ogilby's route, was the main road to the west. In 1577 it was 'the most common travelled way in Cornwall'. Leland went from Camelford to Padstow via Trelill and Wadebridge in Henry VIII's time.

I can only assume the post road went to Padstow to connect with the mails from Ireland – since Padstow had regular trade with Cork. The official post roads described by Ogilby were perhaps not always the routes most frequented by travellers.

For whatever reason, we take Treroosel Road out of St Teath to China Down, and turn left on B3314 to Pendoggett. 'Pertethick' is Port Isaac. We follow B3314, then straight on to St Minver, turning right in the village, then left towards Rock.

…and at 60.4 through St Teath another small village, and 6 furlongs further by several scattering houses on the road; thence at 63.1 you pass by Tregear on the left, and at 63.7 through Peadogget both little villages; then leaving Tresongor House on the right 4 furlongs, you at 65.5 pass through St Indulion alias Endellion a scattering village, and at 68.3 leave St Minver church on the left a furlong.

At 69.5 you pass by some houses on the right called Tredessick and at 70 miles enter on a great sand which is drove (as the people here report) up from the sea by a north-west wind and hath already buried above 300 acres of land, several houses, part of a church yet appearing visible above the sand; near the river you have Predilly church or chapel on the left, and three or four sheds built on the sands for entertainment of people that come for the hurlings and for the direction of passengers.

'I could get no beans for [my horses] till I came back to St Columbe again, which from Truro by St Mitchel was 12 miles, mostly lanes and long miles… From St Columbe I went to Waybridge 6 long miles. Thence to Comblefford, over steep hills 9 miles more; some of this way was over commons of black, moorish ground full of sloughs. The lanes are defended with banks wherein are stones, some great rocks, others slaty stones such as they use for tiling. Comblefford was a little market town, but it was very indifferent accommodations, but the rains that night and next morning made me take up there till about 10 o'clock in the morning; it then made a show of clearing up and made me willing to seek a better lodging.'

Celia Fiennes, 1695

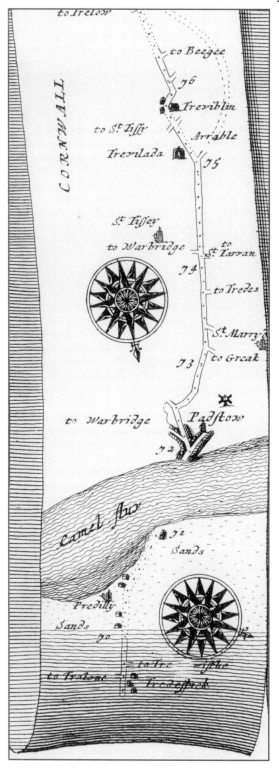

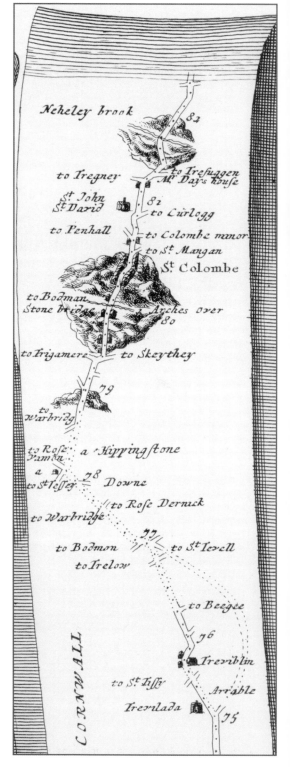

# Padstow - St Columb

We start at Tredrizzick and proceed to what is now called Rock, where at Porthilly (Predilly) Cove we await the ferry for Padstow.

Padstow has been substantially developed, and it is difficult to be sure of the exact route. This contrasts with Gascoyne's 1695 map; following this, a traveller would leave Padstow by B3276, then turn left at Treator crossroads to pick up the A389.

Ogilby's first precisely identifiable point is at 74.1 miles where the A389 now turns left to Little Petherick, which suggests the line of A389 out of Padstow. Yet there is an earlier turning, a Wadebridge road running to the east of our highway: did this ford Little Petherick Creek? If so, it is not shown on Gascoyne's map – but notice the track on the opposite side of the creek (SW926736).

At SW914709 (75.1 miles) the road forks. The direct route goes through Trevillador (SW915706) and Trevibban, after which we can only guess. It is rare for Ogilby to show an alternative route and I suspect the surveyors did not walk the right hand track – the present line of B3274? – which avoided boggy ground. The tracks rejoined around SW915679.

The 'hipping stone' was a stepping stone and was situated on marshy ground near the Cornish Birds of Prey centre. The old road diverged there from today's St Columb by-pass, going west of Tregameer then into St Columb.

We leave St Columb on the White Cross Road through Trekenning.

At 71.2 you come to the River Camel, which rising near Davidstow a small village passes by Camelford and a mile and a half below this place falls into the ocean, and is here 6 furlongs over, and crossed by a ferry to Padstow; a mile and a half below which, in the mouth of the river, is New Island, of note for its good camphire [sic] and sea fowl taken there.

Padstow, a port-town, trading chiefly to Ireland, enjoying several immunities, as sending burgesses to Parliament; hath a good market on Saturdays, no fair, but affording good accommodation.

From Padstow you have St Merryon church on the right and St Tissey on the left, each distant 4 furlongs; at 75.2 you pass Trevilada House on the left and 4 furlongs farther by Treviblin on the right; from whence you go over a large down generally boggy, entering a lane at 78.6 then ascending and descending, and by some straggling houses on the road you at 80 miles over a stone bridge of 2 arches cross a brook or small river, and ascending a furlong farther enter St Columb Major of 3 furlongs extent, containing about 100 houses, which affords very good entertainment, being the usual place where the Justices of the South Division sit; they have privilege of keeping a court once in 3 weeks for all actions under 40 shillings; Sir John Arundel is lord of the town; it hath a good market on Thursdays and one fair yearly, the Thursday after Alhallontide.

At 81 miles you pass by a house on the left called Sir John St David.

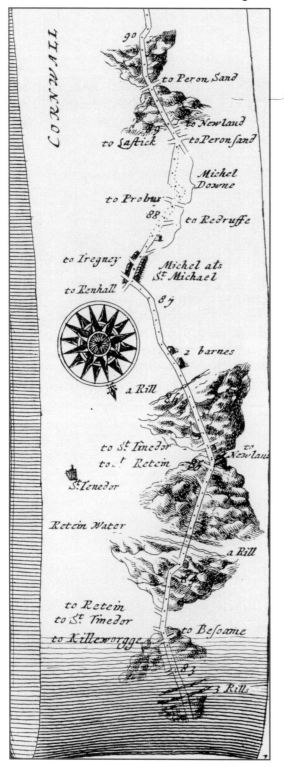

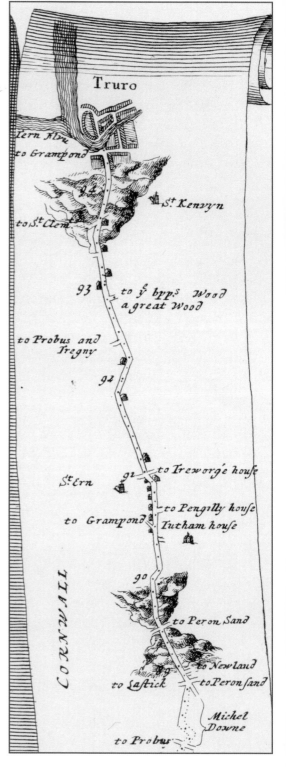

We start around SW 894606. The '3 rills' must, on the modern map, be near the blue 'W' (for well or spring) below the disused quarry. Was 'White Cross' the junction at 83.3 miles? If so, 'Besoame' might be Besoughan (SW 876609). Newquay was of no importance at this time, indeed it is not shown at all on Gascoyne's map except as a settlement called 'Narrow Cliff'. 'Newland' is St Newlyn East.

The cartographer suggests a mountain range lies between St Columb and Mitchell, which, if you follow this attractive section of road, you will find is not actually the case.

The route is then via Luke's Shop (with a left turn to 'Retein' Farm) Gummow's Shop and Tredinnick Farm ('2 barnes') to Mitchell, where the A30 makes a rare appearance in this book. But even one mile of the old A30 is enough for Ogilby. At Carland Cross we turn left alongside a heavily engineered section of A39 which was opened in 1998.

At Buckshead we ignore the blandishments of the modern road and bear right (though a roundabout added in 2003 makes this junction ever more complex!) down the appropriately named Bodmin Road and Mitchell Hill into the City of Truro.

… whence over several hills at 87.2 you enter Michel alias St Michael, a mean town containing about 30 houses, yet sends burgesses to Parliament; has a court leet twice a year, the one half of which is in Newland, and the other is in St Inedar parish; is governed by a portreeve and hath 2 fairs yearly, on St Francis Day and 5 days after Michaelmas.

From St Michael little occurs but passing by Trutham on the right, and St Ern a scattering village on the left; till at 93.4 descending 6 furlongs you enter Truro seated on the River Foy [sic], the chief town of the county, and the place where the Justices of the West Division sit; is large and well built, being a sea port, is well inhabited and frequented, and here likewise the tin is coined; it sends burgesses to Parliament and is governed by a Mayor, Recorder, and 24 Capital Burgesses, out of which 4 are Aldermen chose, and out of them the Mayor; it hath 2 well furnished markets, on Wednesdays and Saturdays, and 4 fairs annually, Wednesday in Whitsun week, the 19th of November, St Thomas' Day and [gap in text].

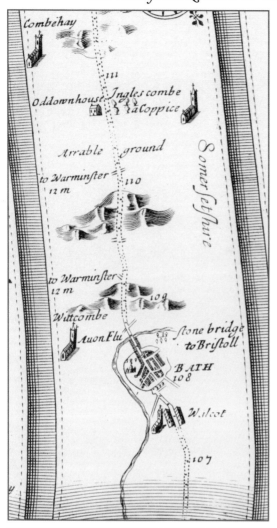

Combehay

Oddownhouse   Inglescombe
                 a Coppice

Arrable     ground
111

to Warminster
12 m          110

*Somersetshire*

to Warminster
12 m

Wittcombe              109

Auon Flu        stone bridge
                to Bristoll

                BATH
                108

                Walcot

                107

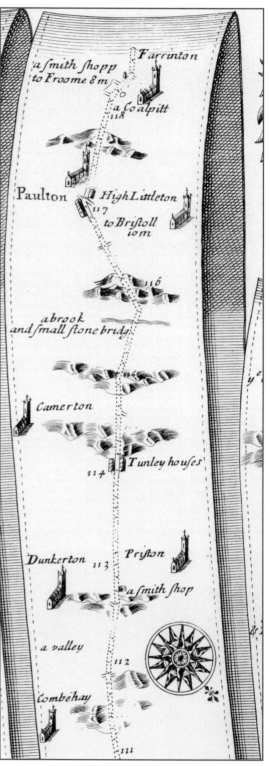

a smith shopp                Farrinton
to Froome 8 m

                a Coalpitt
                118

Paulton      HighLittleton
             117
                to Bristoll
                10 m

                116

abrook
and small stone bridg

Camerton

                Tunley houses
114

Dunkerton   113    Priston

                a smith shop

a valley          112

Combehay

                111

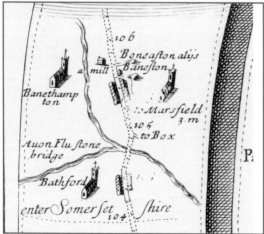

                106
             Boneaston alijs
      a mill   Baneston

Banethamp
ton
             to Marsfield
             105   3 m
                 to Box
Auon Flu stone
   bridge

Bathford

enter Somerset shire
             104

P.

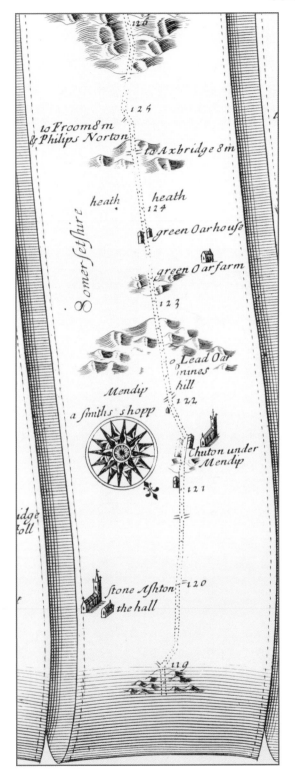

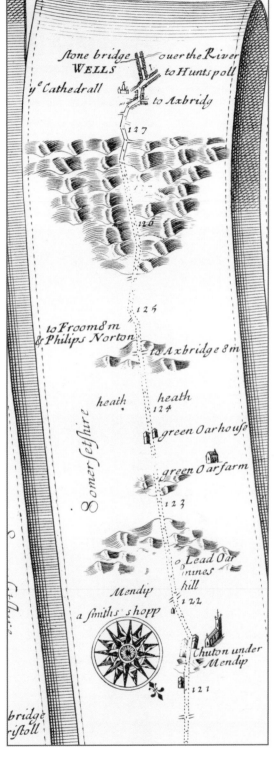

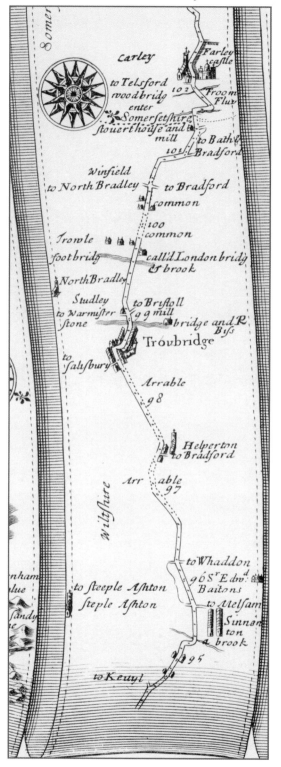

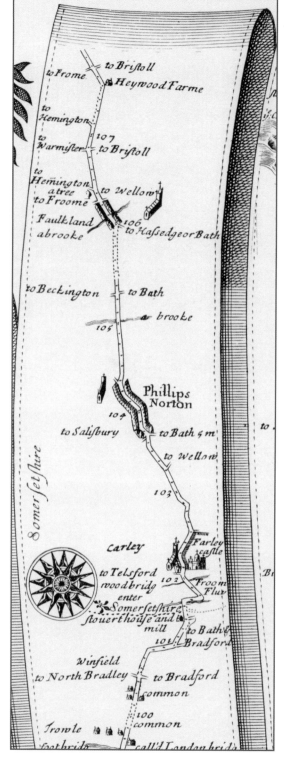

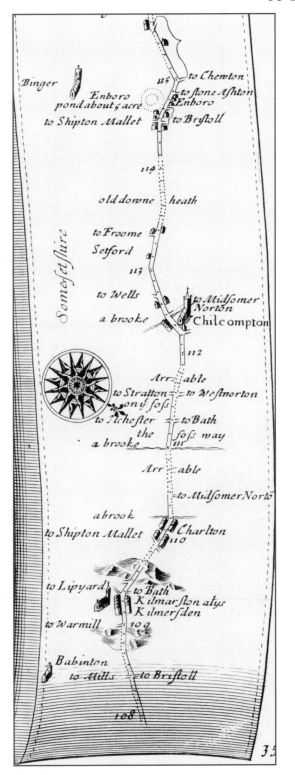

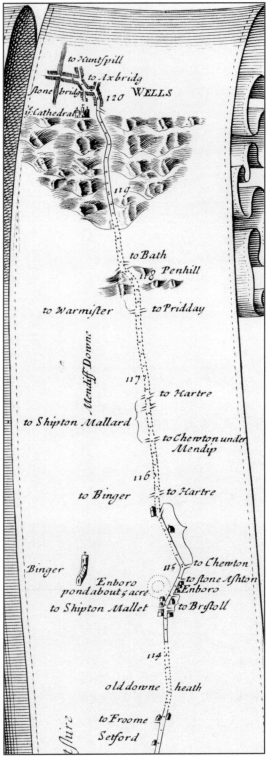

Binger

Enboro
pond about 9 acre
to Shipton Mallet

to Chewton
to stone Ashton
Enboro
to Bristoll

116

114

old downe heath

to Froome
Setford

113

to Wells

a brooke

to Midsomer
Norton
Chilcompton

112

Somersetshire

Arrab able
to Stratton to Westnorton
on ye foss
to Ilchester to Bath
the foss way
a brooke 111

Arrab able

to Midsomer Norto

a brook
to Shipton Mallet

Charlton
110

to Lipyard
to Bath
Kilmarston alys
Kilmersden
to Warmill 109

Babinton
to Mills to Bristoll

108

35

to Huntspill
to Axbridg
stone bridg 120 WELLS
ye Cathedral

119

to Bath
118 Penhill

to Warmister to Pridday

Mendiff Downe

117 to Hartre

to Shipton Mallard

to Chewton under
Mendip

116

to Binger to Hartre

Binger

Enboro
pond about 9 acre
to Shipton Mallet

to Chewton
to stone Ashton
Enboro
to Bristoll

115

114

old downe heath

to Froome
Setford

shire

# The road from Bristol to Exeter

*...in general no ill road, being indifferent well frequented, and everywhere
accommodated with fitting entertainment for travellers.*

## 58A

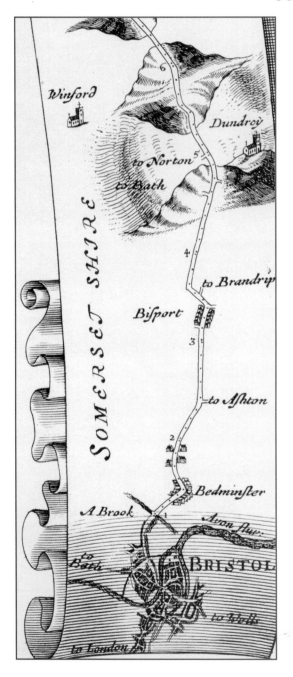

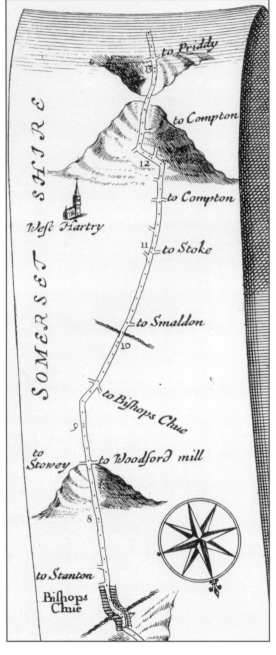

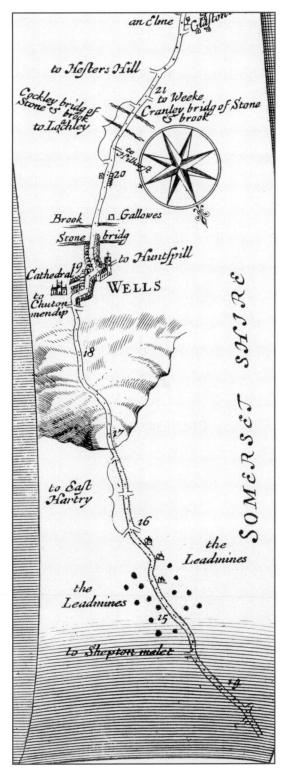

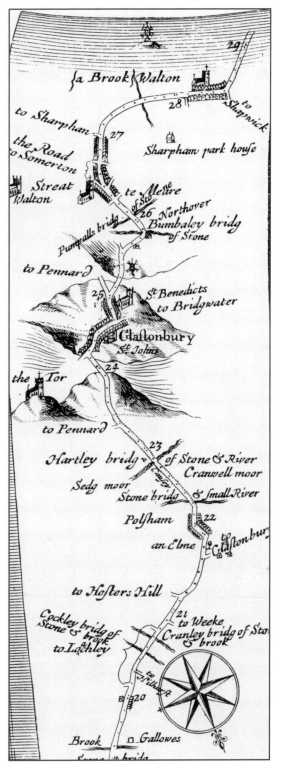

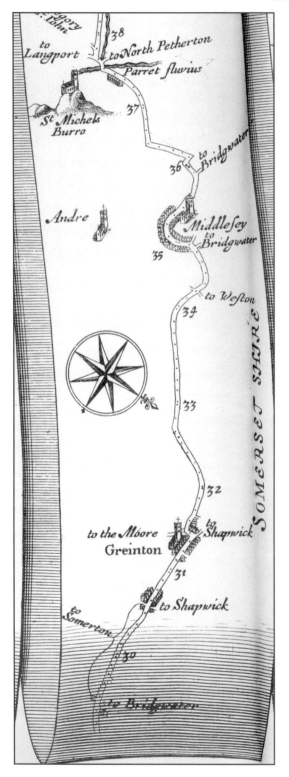

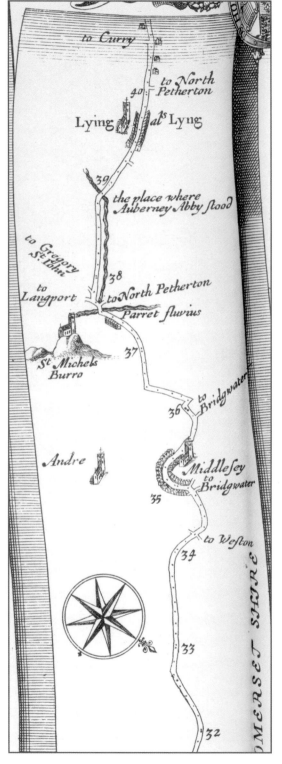

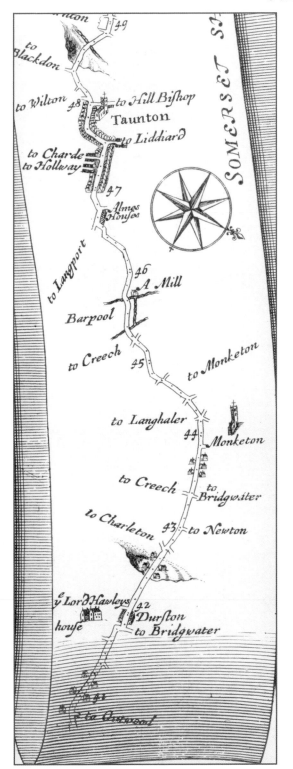

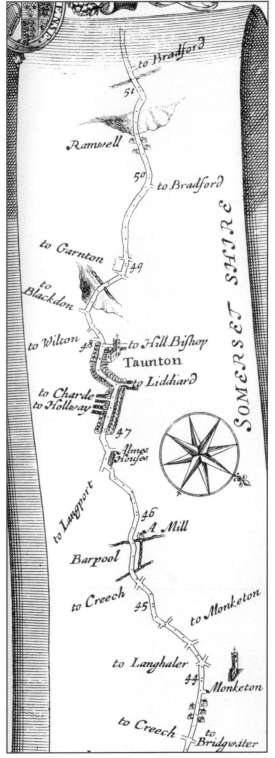

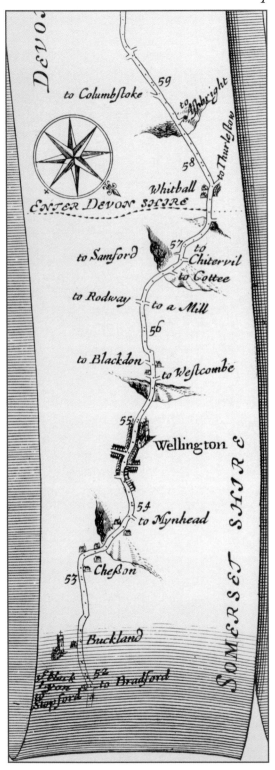

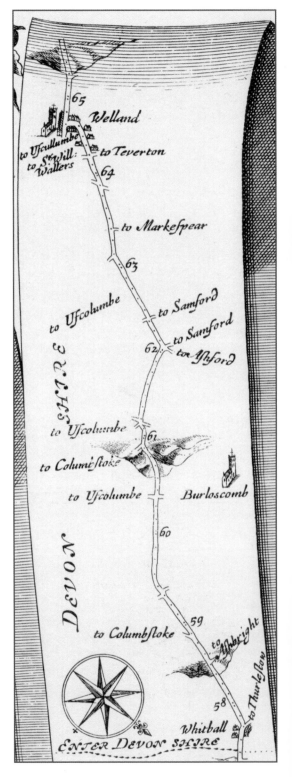

# Wellington

This follows A38 from Taunton to the Chelston roundabout, then into Wellington. The right turn 'to Mynhead' might start you looking for an ancient route across Greedy's Moor to Milverton and on up to Williton for Minehead: perhaps such a route existed, but I think it more probable that the surveyor misheard, or the engraver misread the notes, and that the label should really read 'to Nynehead'.

From Wellington, the route seems to follow the modern A38 surprisingly closely, except at Whiteball, where a truncated track suggests it ascended further up the hill to cut off the corner.

The multiple junction at 61.1 miles is at Appledore. The sharp left turn is at Waterloo Cross where the old A38 is re-numbered B3181. In Willand, we bear left off down to the church, then right along a street which is now called 'Willand Old Village'.

Leaving Taunton you descend a small hill, and at 50.3 pass through Ramwel a little village where you descend again; whence by the Black Lion inn and Buckland church both on the left, pass through Chesson at 53.3 where a small descent conveys you at 54.2 into Wellington, seated on the aforementioned Tone; the town extends 6 furlongs on the road, and hath a small market on Thursdays. Hence 2 repeated descents convey you at 57.4 to the entering Devonshire, 2 furlongs further you pass through Witbal a small village; thence little occurs but passing 2 descents, and by Burloscomb church on the right, till at 64.4 you enter Welland a village of 2 furlongs extent.

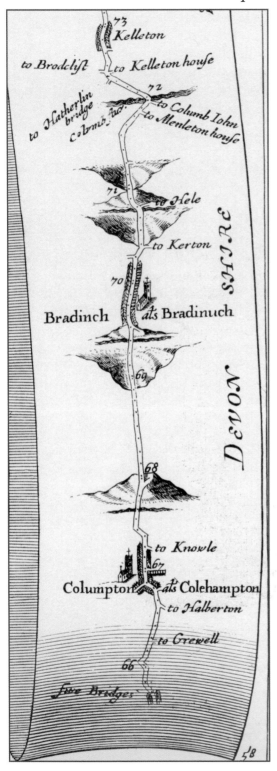

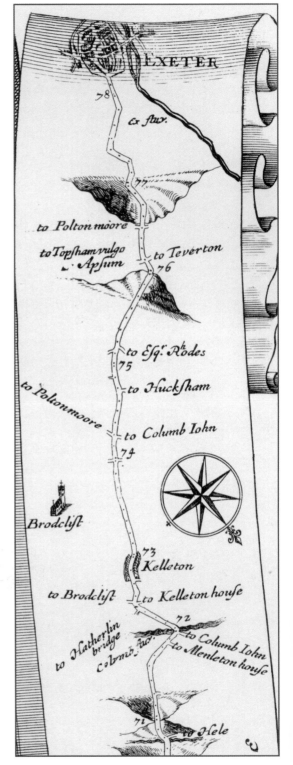

96

# Cullompton - Exeter

From Willand we follow B3181 through Cullompton, then at the end of the town keep straight on, through Bradninch.

The next section I can only explain by assuming there is a small error in Ogilby's map. From Bradninch we start by following the Silverton road, but at SS 990033 we bear left towards Penstone.

The 'Kerton' turn would have taken travellers south of Silverton and across the Exe valley to Thorverton and on to Crediton.

A right turn is shown, 'to Hele': this should have been shown as a left turn. We cross the River Culm at Ellerhayes Bridge, and swing left to pass through Killerton village.

We don't head for Broadclyst, but pass Dane's Wood and Ratsloe to Stoke Post (at 76.1 miles) and enter Exeter by way of Stoke Hill.

From Welland you descend a small hill and pass through Five Bridges a small village, and at 66.6 enter Columpton alias Colehampton extending 4 furlongs on the road; seated near the Columb and has a market on Saturdays. Leaving Columpton you ascend a hill and at 69.3 pass over a vale and a furlong beyond enter Bradinch of 5 furlongs extent, seated likewise on the Columb, which before its devastation by fire enjoyed a market which is now disused. At 70.6 you again cross a vale, and at 71 miles descend a small hill, and a mile farther cross the aforesaid Columb, passing through Kelleton at 72.7 a village of 2 furlongs length, whence by Broadclist church on the left, you ascend a small hill at 75.5 and descend again at 76.4, entering the City of Exeter at 78.2 the account of which you have in London to the Lands End (page 33).

---

'From hence to Exeter we passed much hilly ground and through a very picturesque village of moss-clad houses, called Bradninch… From the summit of Stockhill, two miles from Exeter, you have a glorious circular prospect, the ground gradually falling every way from this centre into a deep and beautiful vale, enriched with various seats, villages, and the fair city…

The common traffic and business of this country is mostly done by horses with panniers and crooks; the former are well-known everywhere but the latter are peculiar to the west, and are simply constructed, with four bent heavy sticks in the shape of panniers, but the ends awkwardly projecting above the rider's head; with these they carry large loads of hay or garden vegetables. The country people ride in a prodigious large boot of wood and leather hung instead of stirrup to the horse's side and half open, which they call gambades.'

Rev. S Shaw, 1788

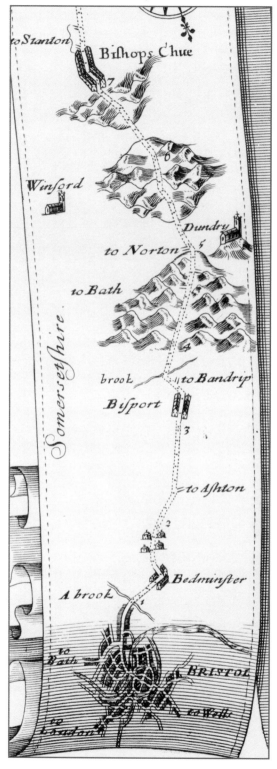

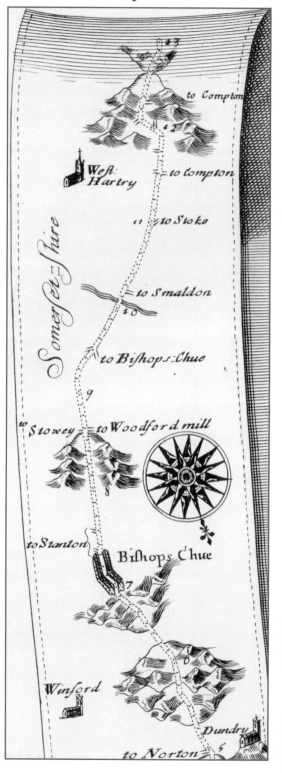

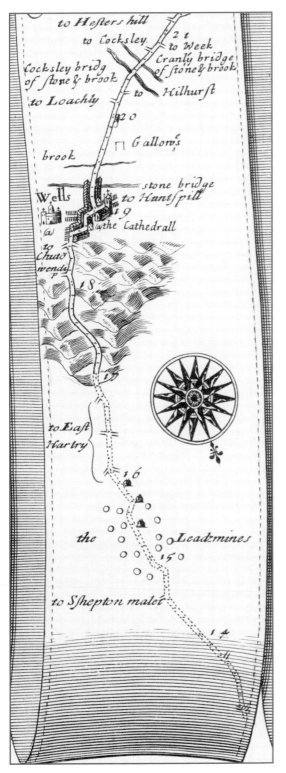

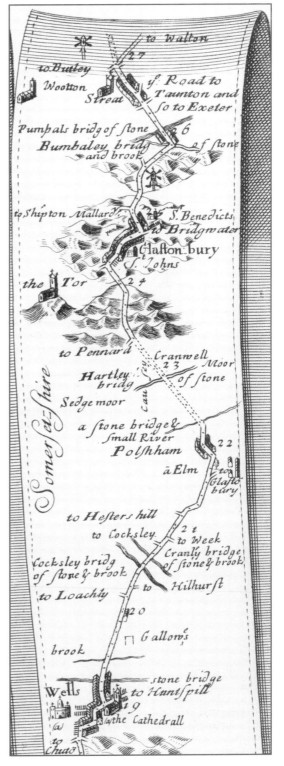

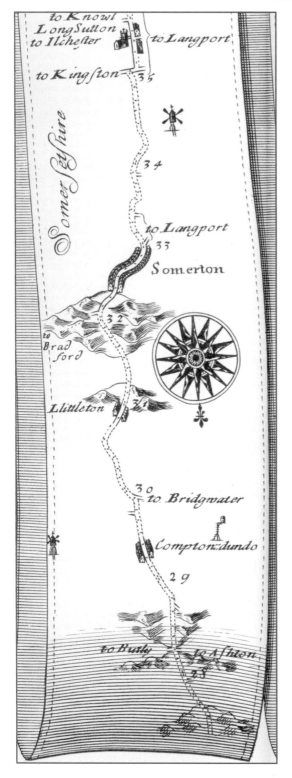

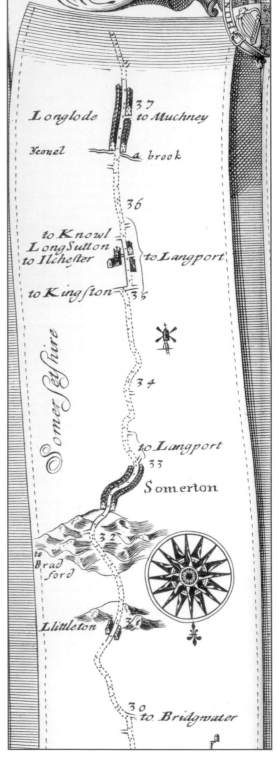

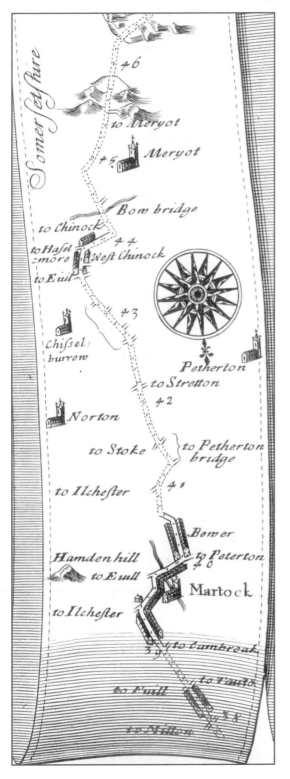

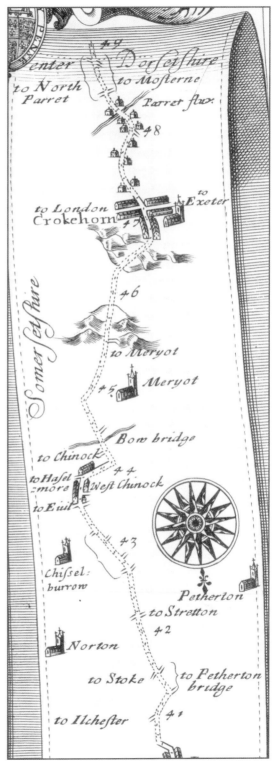

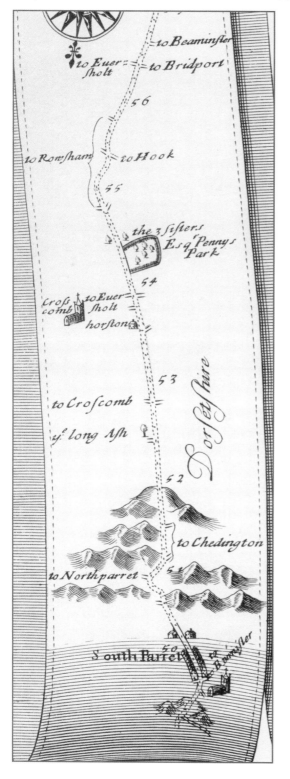

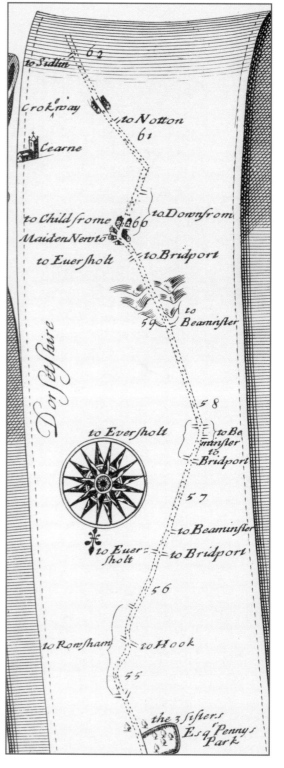

Left strip (bottom to top):

to Beaminster
to Bridport
to Euer ſholt
56
to Rowſham    to Hook
55
the 3 ſiſters
Eſqr Pennys Park
54
Croſſcomb    to Euer ſholt
horſton
53
to Croſcomb
ye long Aſh
52
to Chedington
to Northparret    51
South Parret    50    to Beaminſter
Dorſetſhire

Right strip (bottom to top):

to Sidlin
62
Crokeway
to Notton    61
Cearne
to Childſrome    to Downſrome
Maiden Newto    66
to Euerſholt    to Bridport
to Beaminſter
59
to Everſholt    to Beaminſter
58    to Bridport
57
to Beaminſter
to Euer ſholt    to Bridport
56
to Rowſham    to Hook
55
the 3 ſiſters
Eſqr Pennys Park
Dorſetſhire

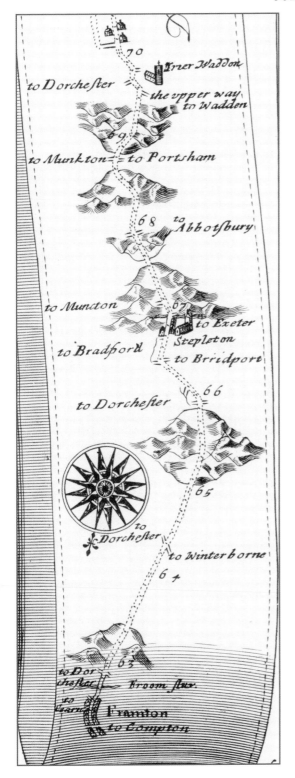

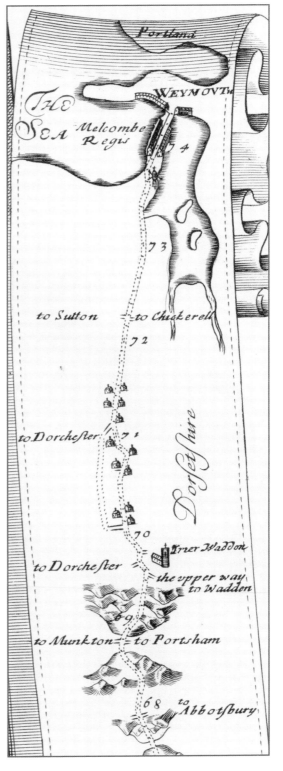

# The road from Dartmouth in Devonshire
## to Minehead in Somersetshire
### 65A    OS Explorer sheets OL20 and 110

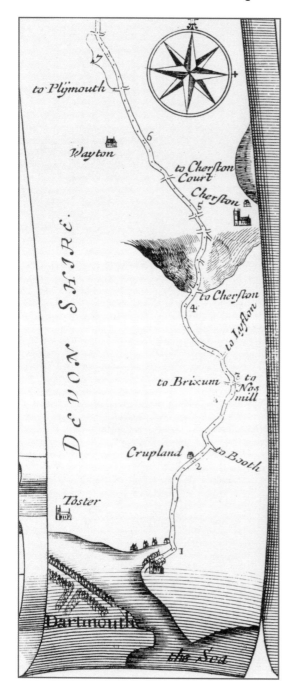

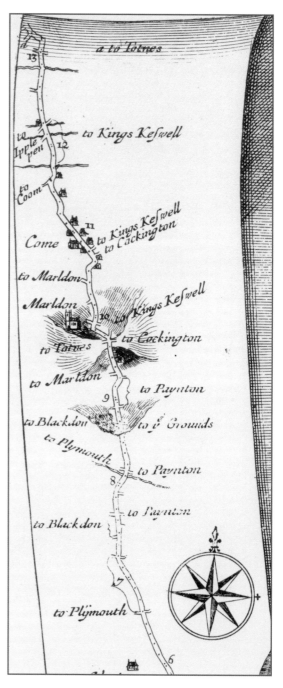

*Affording in general no very good way, as being exceeding hilly,*
*but everywhere replenished with inns etc for entertaining and accommodating*
*travellers; a well frequented road, as being the ready way from Dartmouth*
*a port town on the South Sea to the city of Exeter,*
*and thence to Minehead a port town on the North Sea.*

Starting with the lower ferry to Kingswear, this follows B3205 past Croftland Farm ('Crupland'), Hillhead (where 'Brixum' is incorrectly shown as a left turn) and then by the A379. 'Wayton' is presumably Waddeton.

(Another old road can be followed through Galmpton, Waddeton, past Stoke Gabriel, through Aish, and to Berry Pomeroy. This was the route taken by William of Orange when he landed in 1688, though his army followed the Ogilby route. It can be a handy route from Brixham to Totnes when Torbay becomes congested in summer!)

The A380, which looks at first sight like a 1930s ring road for Paignton, actually predates the resort developments by hundreds of years. Our highway follows the A380 to the roundabout at Churscombe Cross, then goes through Marldon – though its exact line is debatable – to Compton. Torquay, of course, did not yet exist.

At Comptonpool Cross we turn right then bear left, to Abbotskerswell.

Before we proceed to the particulars of the road, take this short view of the initial town. Dartmouth or Dertmouth seated at the mouth of the River Dert, a large, well built, well inhabited and frequented port-town, which is occasioned by its safe and commodious harbour; drives a comfortable trade at sea, and is provided with shipping; it's an ancient Corporation, contains 3 parish churches, enjoying several immunities, as sending burgesses to Parliament, etc, and is governed by a Mayor etc and hath a well furnished market on Fridays.

Leaving the town, you ferry over the Dert (which is here 3 furlongs) and once the other side pass through a village of about 2 furlongs extent, then at 2 miles you pass by Crupland House on the left; at 4.1 descend 5 furlongs and at the bottom leave Cherston church 2 furlongs on the right; whence an indirect way by Wayton House on the left conveys you at 8.6 to a small descent, 3 furlongs farther ascending again, you presently descend 4 furlongs, and on the descent leave Marldon church on the left.

At 10.7 you pass through Come a scattering village, and then by some straggling houses on the road, descend a small hill at 13.3…

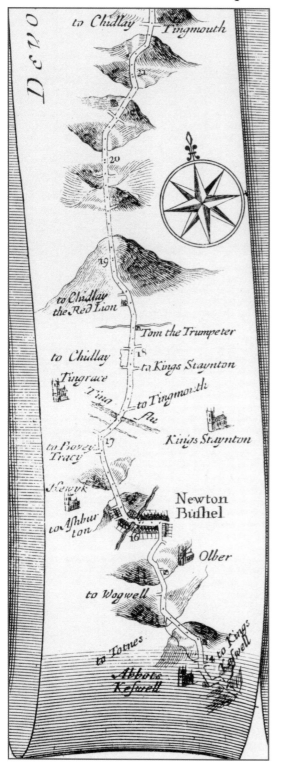

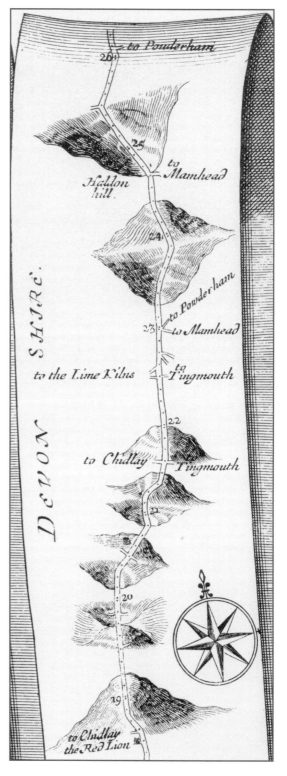

106

From Abbotskerswell we head North, for 'Newton Bushel' – an old name for the northern part of Newton Abbot: the two names confused people for centuries, until Bushel was dropped. We pass between 'Wogwell' (Ogwell) and 'Olber' (Wolborough), probably not by Old Totnes Road (running north from the cemetery) but by the footpath to the church, then the 'other-route-with-public-access' which is a good example of ancient road well preserved and cared for near a town centre.

Following Exeter Road, we cross the Teign. 'Tom the Trumpeter' stood on the site of the present Sandygate Inn at SW 867747, with the 'Red Lion' a few hundred yards beyond it. Perhaps refreshment was required before tackling the hills ahead!

The exact route is now unclear, since Ogilby gives few clues and later road engineering and afforestation have rearranged the landscape. It appears to run close beside or below the A380 to Wapperwell, then to Beggars Bush (are the field boundaries at SW 889789 a fossil road?) and to the double junction, to Powderham and to Mamhead, at SW 904814, after which the line is again uncertain – perhaps through Round Plantation and Woodlands? – to the outskirts of Kennford.

Alternatively, from Sandygate it might have taken the line past Fosterville and Babcombe, then through what became Ugbrooke's parkland.

…and leave Abbots Keswel church on the left; thence ascending 3 furlongs 2 repeated descents by Olber church on the right, leads you at 15.5 into Newton Bushel or Newton Abbots of 5 furlongs extent, seated on the Leman a branch of the Ting or Teing, a town of good accommodation and has a well provided market on Wednesdays for cattle, corn etc. About 5 miles below this town is Tingmouth or Teingmouth, of note for being the place where the Danes first landed.

From Newton Bushel you ascend a small hill, and presently descend again, leaving Hewyk church on the left 2 furlongs; at 17.2 you cross the Ting aforesaid, which rising on the edge of Dartmore near a small village called Gidlay, passes by Chidlay and at Tingmouth aforesaid falls into the sea; then leaving King's Stainton 6 furlongs on the right, and Tingrace 4 furlongs on the left; at 18.2 passing by Tom the Trumpeter's on the right, and 2 furlongs farther by the Red Lion on the left, both inns of accommodation, you ascend a large hill of 6 furlongs; whence over several ascents and descents at 24 miles passing over a large vale and at 27.5 descending Haldon Hill of 7 furlongs…

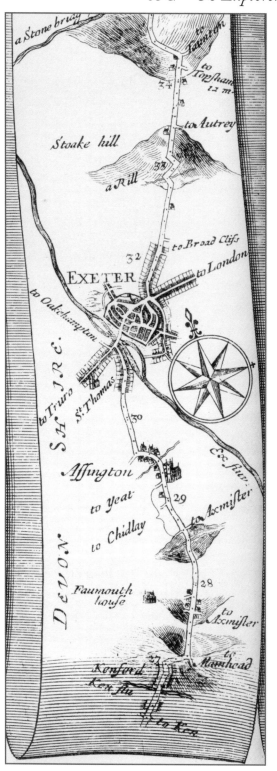

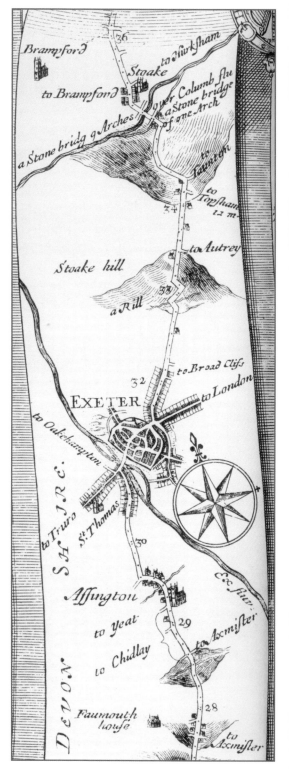

From Kennford towards 'Affington' there are turnings right to 'Axminster', which is Exminster – not a ferry route into East Devon. The map of Exeter is particularly clear and attractive.

The Tiverton-Minehead highway leaves, appropriately, by way of Old Tiverton Road, then Stoke Hill and Stoke Canon Bridge, where it becomes the present A 396, to Rewe.

I can recommend an exploration of this route by car, particularly from Tiverton to Minehead, the Rewe-Tiverton section being just a trifle narrow in places, even by my standards!

... brings you at 26.6 to cross the small River Ken (which about 4 miles below falls into the Ex) where ascending you enter Kenford of 2 furlongs extent; thence 2 repeating descents passing through a scattering village, and leaving Falmouth House 2 furlongs on the left, leads you at 28.4 over a vale.

At 29.4 you pass through Affington a scattering village, and at 30.2 enter the suburbs of Exeter, and over the bridge enter the city, which we have illustrated in previous plates; at the leaving the city you omit the great road that leads to London etc, and bear to the left through a suburb of 4 furlongs extent.

At 32.7 crossing a rill you ascend Stoke Hill of 5 furlongs, and by some scattering houses at 34 miles, a descent of a mile conveys you to a stone bridge of 9 arches over the River Columb just at its confluence with the Ex; 2 furlongs farther you pass through Stoke a small village, and leave Brampford church on the right 4 furlongs;

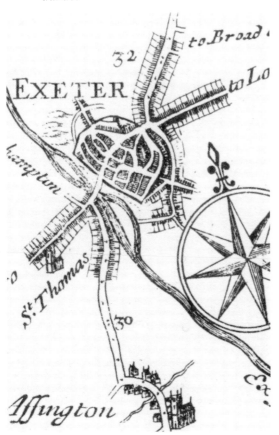

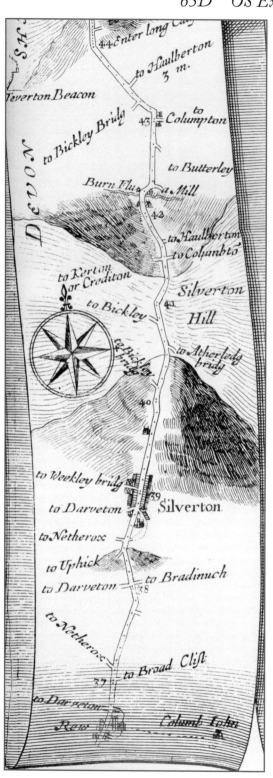

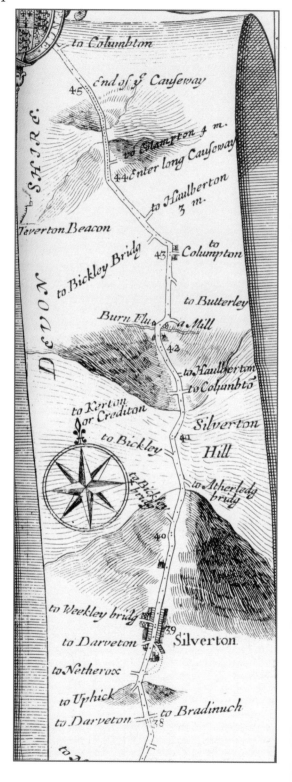

From Rewe we follow A 396 but soon bear right to Stumpy Cross (where 'Darveton' is Thorveton) and into Silverton, which is seen as a town on a north-south axis: contrast this with the modern map. Has the village changed dramatically since the Exeter-Tiverton road migrated west, or is it just in the eye of one or both cartographers?

A steep climb takes us to Ash Farm and north to Figtree Farm. (The later turnpike, through Bickleigh, avoided these hills.) From Figtree Farm, the other-route-with-public-access is, as so often, the line of the ancient highway, descending an incline more suitable for pedestrians and horses than for wheeled traffic.

At the Burn River a right turn, then first left, heading for Tiverton by way of Exeter Hill – yet another road name which confirms we have found the old route.

The Long Causeway would have stretched from Borough Farm to Holwell Combe. This mile of well paved road in the middle of the countryside was clearly most unusual for the post roads of Devon, and it would be interesting to know how it came to be there.

… and at 36.4 through Rew a scattering village; then at 38.1 you ascend a small hill, and at 38.6 enter Silverton a good town of accommodation, 3 furlongs in extent; governed by a portreeve and hath 2 fairs annually, Midsomer Day and St Bartholomew.

At the end of the town you ascend Silverton Hill which is a mile and a half on the road, descending it again at 41.2; 8 furlongs and at the bottom cross the Burn a small brook, then at 43 miles by some houses on the right, and at 44 miles ascending, you come upon Long Causeway of a mile extent well paved;

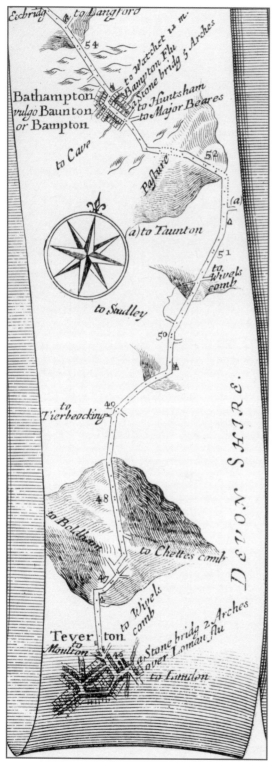

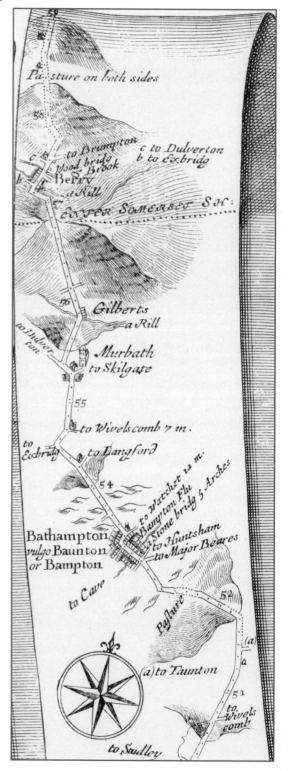

# North from Tiverton

Within Tiverton, we seem to take Station Road, Barrington Street, and Park Road, streets on which the modern town turns its back. On Sheet 114 this is the route between 'Hosp' and 'Sch' and north past 'Cemy', taking the footpath under A361, then turning right to skirt Knightshayes, over Vanpost Hill, past Sparkhayne, then bearing left into Bampton. The Exe Valley road, now A396, did not exist until 1819.

The route through Bampton seems clear, leaving by B3190, but the present alignment between Bampton and Morebath bears little relation to the angles shown by Ogilby. (By contrast, Donn in 1765 shows the present route.) Ogilby's road has for once apparently left no trace on the map – unless it was appropriated for the railway branch line?

From Morebath we go through Hayne Cross, along a classic holloway to Bury, descending a very steep hill where even the old route required a right-angle bend. Bury is a wonderfully quiet and attractive backwater with a ford and narrow stone 'pack-horse bridge' – yet Ogilby's map tells us the bridge in his day was still of wood. North of Bury we climb steeply, perhaps even more directly than the present bridleway since no zig-zag is shown in 1675, to the Tower on Bury Hill, joining the modern road at SS937287.

...then after a small descent at 45.5 you enter Teverton or Twerton, *q.d.* Twyford Town, as being seated at the confluence of the Leman with the Ex, a large town, containing above 500 houses, and hath much suffered by fire; it at present drives a considerable trade in clothing, enjoying several privileges, as sending burgesses to Parliament, hath 2 good free schools and 3 almshouses; is governed by a Mayor, Recorder, 12 Elders and 12 Assistants; hath a considerable market on Tuesdays and 2 fairs annually, the Tuesday sevennight after Whitsunday, and Michaelmas Day.

From Teverton you pass over a large valley, and after 3 repeated descents are conveyed at 53 miles to Bath-Hampton *vulgo* Bampton or Baunton, of 4 furlongs extent, seated on a branch of the Ex, and in a bottom environed with hills; it numbers above 100 houses, and has a large church where are entombed several members of the family of the Earls of Bath; it's governed by a portreeve, and had formerly 2 markets weekly, Wednesdays and Saturdays, but now only one and that on Mondays, with 2 fairs yearly, Whitsun Tuesday and St Luke's Day.

At 54 miles you descend a small hill, and at 55.2 pass through Murbath a small village and presently a descent of 3 furlongs (by Gilberts on the right) is seconded by an ascent of 8 furlongs at the top of which you enter Somersetshire, and presently descending a steep hill at 57.2 pass through Berry a small village, whence over 2 large ascents over Brunnam Hill...

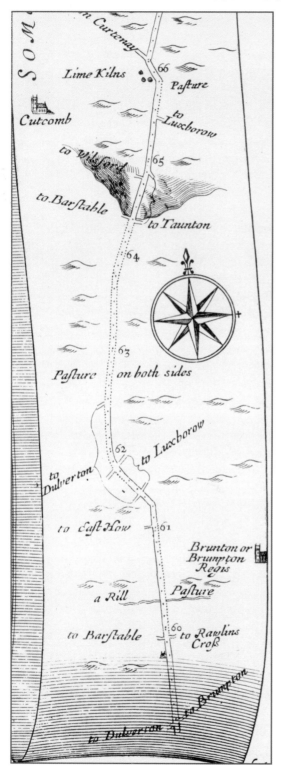

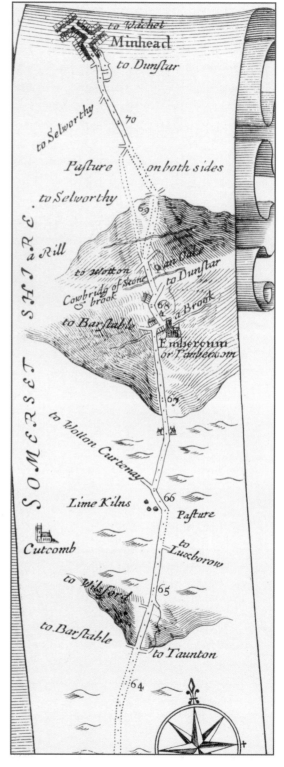

# North to Minehead

We cross the route of the Bridgwater to Barnstaple post-road (see page 65).

This section generally follows a modern minor road parallel to A396 but following the ridge to the east rather than the valley.

The pair of turnings to 'Luxburow' are at Stolford Hill Cross and Broad Lane Head, and the Barnstaple-Taunton road at Heath Poult Cross. This cross-road must be an ancient Saxon road: note that to the north-west it is labelled 'Hare Path', from the Old English for 'army-road' – the A-roads of their day. The next 'Luxburow' turning is at Couple Cross. (There are no changes of direction at this point: so did Ogilby's road go over Kersham Hill?)

The Wootton Courtenay turning will be Slade Lane (SS952395). After Beasley we take the footpath route into Timbercombe and from there we cross Cow Bridge, after which Ogilby's has two alternative routes running through 'pasture on both sides' in contrast with today's forestry.

Perhaps he took a more or less direct course from Cowbridge Cross to Higher Hopcott (SS963461). The exact entry into Minehead is obscured by later development. On a modern street plan of Minehead, however, the line of Hopcott Path looks promising: it is shown as part of the 'Macmillan Way' on the OS map, just north of Lower Hopcott.

… whence over 2 large ascents over Brunnam Hill being generally open, heathy and furze ground, little occurs but passing by Brumpton Regis a mile on the right, till at 64.3 you descend 4 furlongs and leave Cutcombe church on the left.

Then at 65.7 you pass by some lime kilns on the left and at 66.7 descending a large hill, you pass through Embercumb or Timbercomb a village of good accomodation; whence ascending 7 furlongs through open way, at 70.6 you enter Minhead a Borough and port-town, whose convenient harbour occasions an indifferent trade to Ireland etc. It elects Parliament men and has a small market on Wednesdays.

# The road from Exeter to Barnstaple
## continued to Ilfarcomb in Devonshire
*Generally a rough hard way, yet wants not a fitting reception for travellers.*

### 68A    OS Explorer sheets 114 and 113

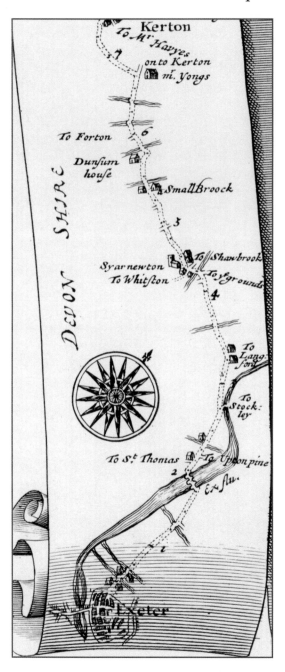

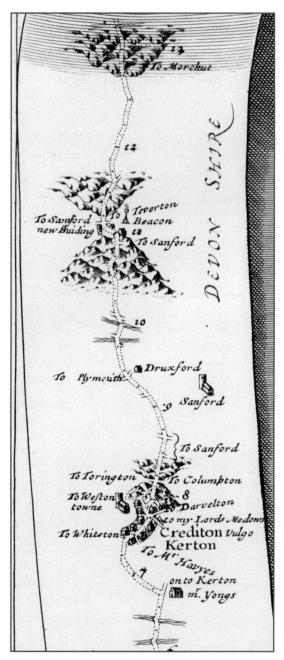

# Exeter - Crediton

Leaving Exeter by North Street through St Davids, we cross Cowley Bridge and follow A 377 through Newton St Cyres and Dunscombe. Was 'Mr Yong's house' Downes, or Downes Home Farm? The present house Downes apparently dates from the 1690s and was the home of the Gould family in the early eighteenth century. Instead of taking the direct route, through Downes Home Farm and the footpath, Ogilby turns sharp left (at SX 847999?) and near the station rejoins A 377 to enter Crediton.

The Crediton-Barnstaple road did not take its present A377 route along the Taw valley until 1830.

Within Crediton Ogilby's route heads north, passing to the east of the church, turns briefly left along Blagdon (the 'Darvelton' turning is Old Tiverton Road). Then he heads north-west, up Jockey Hill or Deep Lane to Forches Cross, keeping left at Frogmire (SS 827015).

The route now runs to the south of Ruxford Barton, through Cross Hill and New-buildings (still so-called more than three centuries later!) and Oldborough.

From Exeter, first passing 2 or 3 small rills, you cross the Ex at 1.6 having a little above received the Credy, and passing another rill, you touch upon the aforesaid Credy, crossing 2 rills more, and at 4.3 pass through Syar Newton, alias Newton Syres, a small village near the banks of the Credy; whence over 3 other rills, and by Dunsum House on the left, you at last cross the Forton and at 7.3 enter Crediton *vulgo* Kerton, seated on the west of the Credy at a little distance, near its conjuction with the Forton; a large town, extending 5 furlongs on the road, divided into the east and west towns; hath a great market on Saturdays, a good trade for serges, shews a fair church, formally the Bishop's See, with an incorporated free school; and is of note for giving birth to Winifred the apostle of the Hussians etc in Germany.

At the end of the town you pass over a small hill, and crossing 2 rills at 10.3 ascend an hill of 6 furlongs at the top of which you pass through New Buiding ['Buidings' in the margin] a small village, presently descending for half a mile;

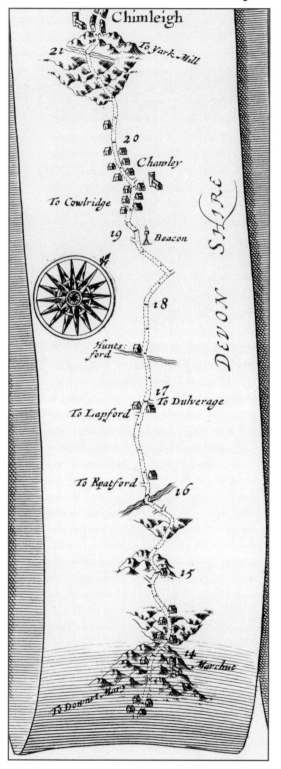

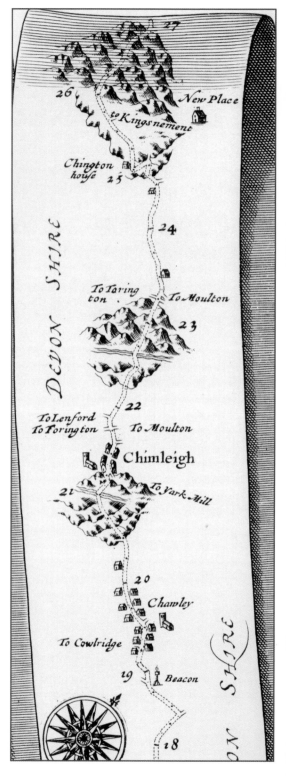

## Morchard Bishop - Chittlehamholt

Starting at Frost, we keep left as we go through Morchard Bishop ('Marchut') then keep right at Turning Ways to Eastington and continue north-west.

'Huntsford' is now Handsford (SS729105). At Labbetts Cross we turn left onto B3042, cut a corner via a footpath, go through Chawleigh (was it really so extensive in 1675?) and follow B3096 into Chulmleigh.

From Chulmleigh we head north-north-west by way of Bonds Cross and Trunk Bridge to cross the River Mole at Head Bridge (SS667183) and follow B3226 to Chittlehamholt.

…whence an unlevel way, succeeded by a more fertile vale, wherein you cross 2 or 3 branches of the Taw, brings you, by the beacon on the right, to Chawley at 19.2 a discontinued village of 4 furlongs; whence crossing a valley, and therein a branch of the Taw; on the top of the ascent at 21.2 you enter Chimleigh or Chulmleigh, a small market town of 2 furlongs length, seated at the confluence of the foresaid water with the Taw.

At 22.5 in a valley you cross another branch of the foresaid Taw, ascending 4 furlongs and passing by Chington House on the left at 25 miles, thence descending easily to 26 miles, you have a more eminent rise for near a mile…

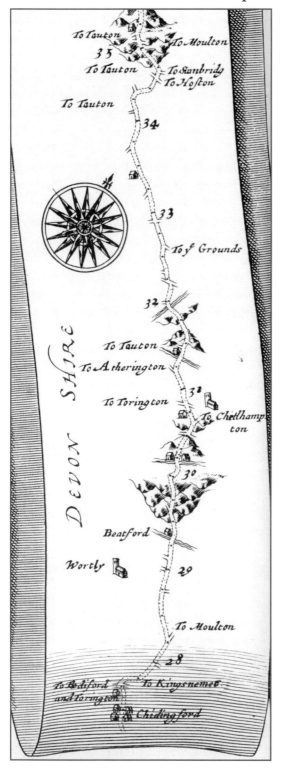

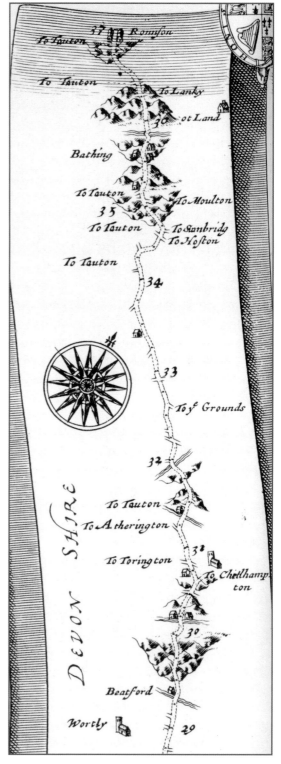

# Chittlehamholt - Barnstaple

Starting at Chittlehamholt ('Chiddingford') we bear left at Cockrams Butt Cross, pass Swing Gate Cross, then skirt Chittlehampton (though I can recommend that both the village and church deserve a visit, if you are following the road on the ground), turn right at Biddacott Cross and head for Higher Cobbaton, before Traveller's Rest (perhaps a defunct posting house?), Halmpstone Cross and Hearson Cross, and through Bableigh ('Bathing') to SS 591300. From here we enter Barnstaple by Venn Road and Newport.

…which carries you at 27.2 through Chidingford a small village; thus leaving Wortley 3 furlongs on the left, you cross a small rill, by Beatford House contiguous on the left descend 4 furlongs, pass another rill at 30.1 and leaving Chetelhampton church a small distance on the right. At 30.6 cross 2 small rills, pass through Bathing at 35.5 and Ronson at 37 miles, both small villages.

At 37.2 you enter Newport of 4 furlongs extent, where you fall in with the road from Bridgwater…

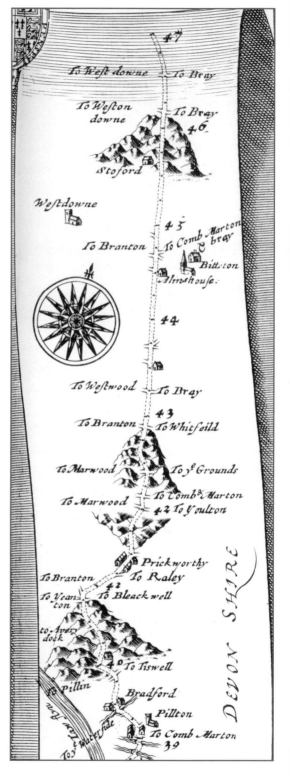

# Barnstaple - Ilfracomb

Just occasionally, studying Ogilby is of some practical modern use. His route from Barnstaple to Ilfracombe is an interesting alternative to the two more obvious routes, especially if there's a burst water main in Braunton at the peak of the holiday season.

Follow Barnstaple's town wall round from Long Bridge and cross the Yeo by the Lynton Road. Turn left immediately after the bridge, then take the third right, Abbey Street, into Pilton – which was the original Saxon burh or fortified settlement, losing out to the upstart Barnstaple in the tenth century.

Go through Bradiford, up Upcott Hill, then bear right at the fork (the left fork goes to Braunton, another useful August route) and bear right again to Prixford ('Prickworthy'), keeping left to Wigley Cross, then across Swindon Down by a very straight road into 'Ilfarcomb'.

Ogilby shows it as passing through unenclosed land, which explains why it is so straight.

At 37.2 you enter Newport of 4 furlongs extent, where you fall in with the road from Bridgwater, 3 furlongs beyond which you enter Barstable or Barnstaple at 38.1 a large and well frequented corporation and market town (for which see page 69). The main body of the town lies on the right, extending only 3 furlongs upon this road; 4 furlongs beyond which (first crossing 2 small rills, branches of the adjacent Taw) you pass through Pilton and 3 furlongs farther Bradford, both small villages.

At 40 miles you ascend for 6 furlongs, pass through Prickworthy a small village, and crossing a valley at 42 miles, leave Bittaden 3 furlongs on the right, passing by Stowford at the bottom of another ascent of 5 furlongs, descending at 48 miles for 4 furlongs, and at 48.7 entering Ilfarcomb *vulgo* Ilfracomb, a good market town, situate on the shore of the Severn Sea, almost opposite to Swanzey in Glamorganshire, enjoying a safe harbour for ships.

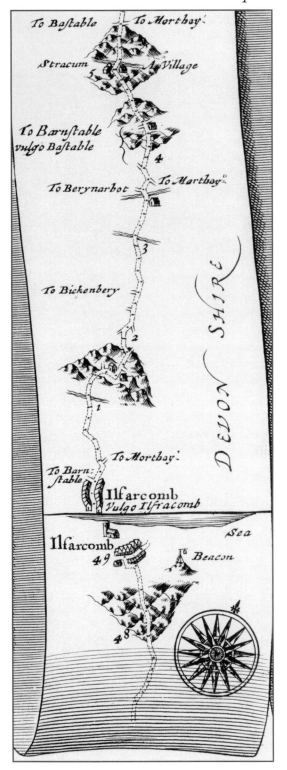

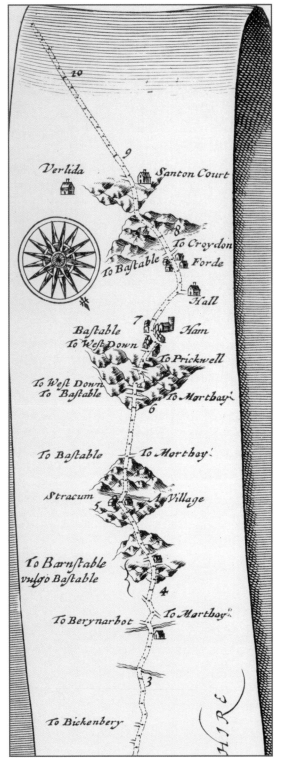

# Ilfracombe - Braunton Burrows

How useful it would be to have a modern Ilfracombe-Bideford route which avoids Barnstaple, as Ogilby does. But alas his route has one major defect!

He leaves the town by Slade Road. From Upper Slade a footpath cuts a corner on the way towards Turnpike Cross. 'Bickenbury' is Bickenbridge. South of Turnpike Cross (which on Ogilby's map is at 3.6 miles from Ilfracombe) a field boundary indicates the decayed line of the old road, which then heads south down Hartnall's Lane to Spreacombe, Oxford Cross and Georgeham ('Ham'), then through Forda and by way of a bridleway (Hannaburrow Lane) to Saunton. 'Verlida' must be Fairlinch.

Donn in his map of 1765 also shows this route; Braunton Burrows seem to have extended further west. The route roughly follows today's coast path to the (then) southern tip of the Burrows. Donn shows St Anne's Chapel as in ruins.

From Ilfarcomb beginning anew our computation, you first cross a small rill at 1 mile, ascending for 5 furlongs, passing 2 other rills and over a small vale, and coming at 5 miles to Stracum a small village, seated on a rivulet in a bottom. At 6 miles a descent of 6 furlongs leads you into Ham of 2 furlongs extent; whence through Ford a small village at the bottom of an ascent, and by Santon court on the left...

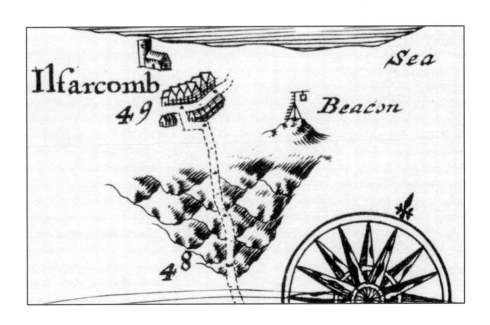

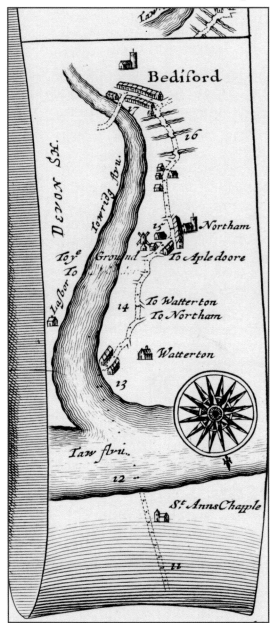

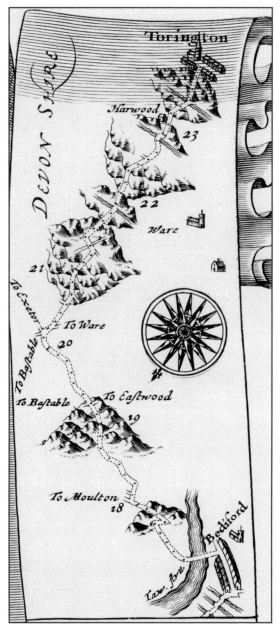

# Braunton - Bideford - Torrington

From the Burrows Ogilby's surveyors crossed by ferry to Appledore, a good mile and surely difficult at some stages of the tide.

After briefly following A386 we keep right into Northam, past the church, and by way of Fore Street rejoin A386 to the roundabout. At the foot of Heywood Road we keep right along Northam Road and North Road, which becomes Mill Street, now pedestrianised. This was very much Bideford's main street in 1675. We cross the bridge.

The very abrupt change of compass direction now requires Ogilby to break this section into two parts, which is unusual – though convenient for our small format volume.

The exact route up the hill at East-the-Water, with its sharp dog-leg, is unclear. Donn in 1765, by which time East-the-Water had streets and buildings which it apparently lacked in 1675, starts by heading south down Torrington Street, then sharp left up Torrington Lane. Ogilby clearly does something different, but his path may have been built over.

We soon pick up the present road to Gammaton Moor, where we turn right for Torrington via Norwood ('Harwood').

… on the other side of the hill you come at 11.4 to St Ann's Chapel on the right, and 3 furlongs farther by a ferry above a mile cross the Taw at its conjunction with the Towridg.

At 14.6 you go through Northam of 3 furlongs extent, seated on the banks of the Towridg, whence crossing several little waters, at 16.4 you enter Bediford or Bytheford, seated on the foresaid Towridg, over which it hath a large stone bridge of 24 arches, so high that ships of 60 tun may pass under; a large and flourishing town, well inhabited and frequented, enjoying a good trade, with a well provided market on Tuesdays.

From Bediford you take your way over the bridge, an irregular road, ascending at 17.5 for 3 furlongs, and at 18.5 for 5 furlongs, bringing you to a descent at 20.5 of 5 furlongs, whence by repeated ascents and descents, over 2 or 3 rills, a hard stony way conveys you at 23.7 to Torrington Magna, a large market town seated on the foresaid Towridg (for which see page 71).

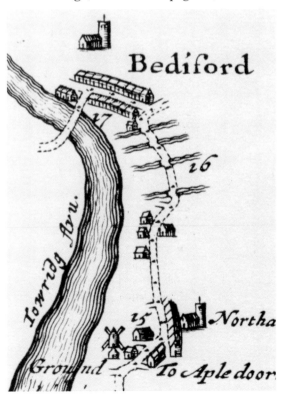

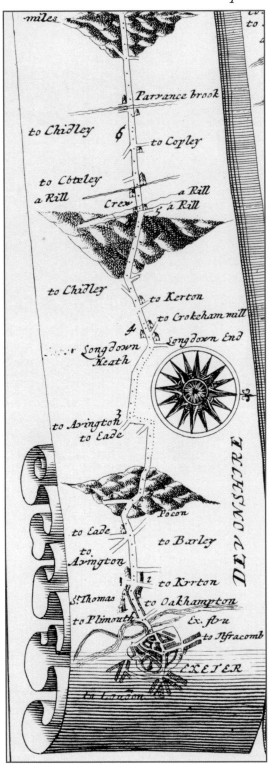

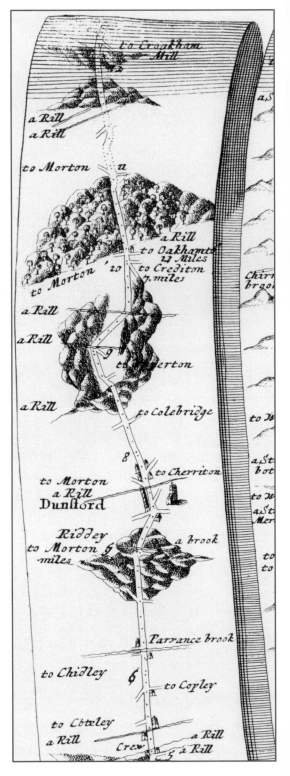

# The road from Exeter to Truro in Cornwall

*...affording an indifferent good road to Chagford though hilly, but after over Dartmoor to Tavistock exceeding bad, being hilly, boggy and stony, without any accommodation; but then to Truro indifferent good again, being everywhere (except on Dartmoor) furnished with good inns of accommodation.*

We leave Exeter by B3212 (Cowick Street) and follow it to Longdown. Shortly after Perridge Cross, we take the short cut to Midwinter Cottages and rejoin B3212. 'Parrance Brook' is now Sowton Brook at Farrants Bridge.

At Reedy, the Moreton turn is B3212: we go over the bridge into and through Dunsford. At Butts we keep left, leaving sheet 114 at SX800895.

The next section is more than a little mysterious, in that the River Teign is not shown. It must surely have been crossed at Clifford Bridge, which should be at about 10.0 miles from Exeter. The turning to Moreton at that point could be the lane from Clifford Bridge via Mardon Down.

The line of Boyland Road does not agree with Ogilby's alignments: perhaps there was a more direct path now lost.

From Clifford Bridge it is 3 miles to Uppacott Farm (SX733885), which is shown  as 'Upcot' at 13.0 miles, tending to confirm my guess.

From the great conduit in Exeter you take your way to the West Gate, where over a fair stone bridge you cross the navigable River Ex, which rising on Exmoor passes by Teverton and this place; receiving into it first the Dunsbrook and therein the Barle, second the Leman, third the Columb and therewith the Wever, fourth the Credy and therein the Forton, fifth the Clyst and sixth the Ken, falling into the sea at Exmouth. At the end of the bridge you enter St Thomas a suburb of Exeter. Extending 4 furlongs on the road, whence at 2 miles you cross a brook in a vale, where you pass by some houses called Pocon, and enter on Longdown Heath; at 3.7 you leave the heath and pass through a village called Longdown End, and at 4.4 descend 5 furlongs, passing in the bottom through a little village called Crew.

Hence at 7 miles you cross a vale and leave Reddey a village contiguous on the left, and at 7.5 through Dunsford a long scattering village, at 8.3 you descend 3 furlongs and pass through a large vale, ascending at 10.1 6 furlongs, then at 11.5 you ascend...

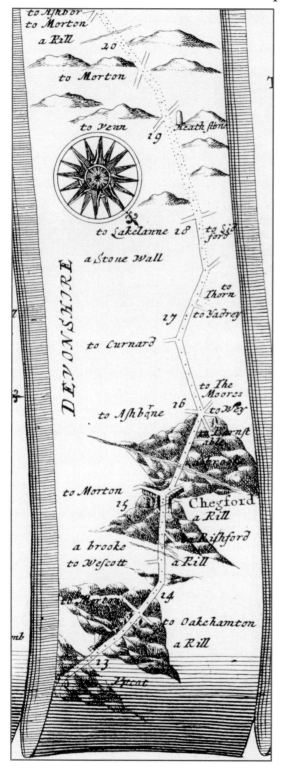

# Over Dartmoor

From Uppacot we cross Ogilby's Okehampton-Moreton road (now A382) at Easton and enter Chagford by B3206; we turn right at the square then bear left down Manor Road.

In front of Waye Barton we keep left past Tunnaford; the right turn to 'Yadrey' (Yardworthy) is now part of the Two Moors Way.

'Thorn' is Thornworthy. We now join the Two Moors Way across Chagford Common.

The old road joins the later turnpike (the Act was passed in 1772 but the actual road and the new bridges were many years in construction) at the Warren House Inn, 19 miles 5 furlongs from Exeter.

At 19.0 miles Ogilby says we pass on the right 'a stone for direction' called the Heath Stone. The Heath Stone is referred to in old documents as a boundary marker. There has been much learned debate about it over the last century or more, which I am not competent to judge. The OS map places the Heath Stone at SW671837. I calculate that Ogilby places it around SW673825 – where there happens to be a prominent standing stone at the end of a stone row – a useful landmark by the track. This is the stone the surveyor saw and which he identified, rightly or wrongly, as the Heath Stone.

Clapper bridges at Postbridge and by the Powder Mills ('Chirrey brooke') are mentioned, as is one at Two Bridges.

… and 2 repeated descents convey you through a valley; and at 14.4 you descend [*recte* ascend] a hill on which is seated Chegford, formerly a market town now disused; it at present contains about 80 houses, and is graced with a fair church in which are the tombs of Sir William Whiddon and James Prouz Esquire; about 3 miles distant on the left is Morton or Morton Hampsteed, which enjoys a good market on Saturdays.

Leaving Chegford you cross a brook in a vale, and enter on Dartmoor at 17.3 whence little occurs but bad way, at 19 miles you have a stone for direction on the right called Heath-Stone, and at 20.4 you cross Turnabout Brook, and 2 furlongs farther you have a stone on the left called Merrey Pit, and 5 furlongs beyond that a house on the right of the same name; then at 21.7 you cross a stone bridge of 3 arches called Postbridg over a brook, and at 23.4 you cross another stone bridge over Cherrey Brook; thence passing by Crockham Tor on the right, a hill of rocks so called, at 25.3 over a stone bridge you cross the Dart…

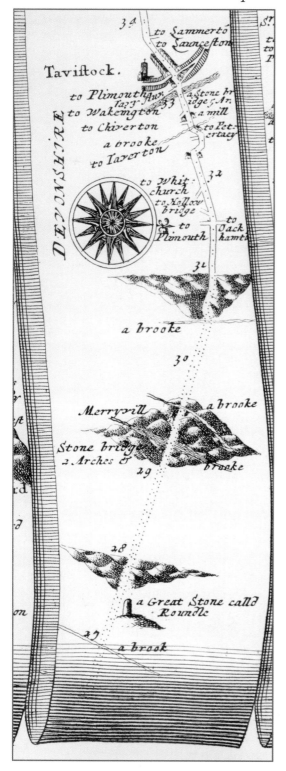

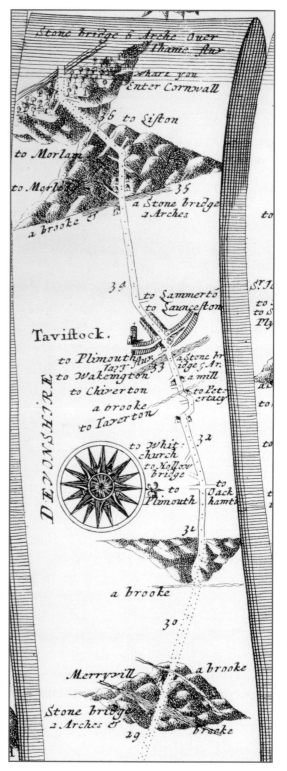

# Tavistock

The Rundle Stone was an ancient boundary marker, a 'pillar' more than 7 ft tall and 4 ft in girth, which was destroyed in the 1880s. Note the absence of the Rundlestone to Princetown road. From the Rundlestone to Tavistock, the route seems little changed except for its straightness, especially at Merrivale.

The Plymouth-Okehampton road crosses our route at Moorshop: it was then the main north-south route for West Devon, leaving A396 at Horrabridge, passing through Moorshop to Peter Tavy and Mary Tavy, missing out Tavistock. Donn's map of 1765 still shows the Moorshop route as more important than the Tavistock route.

The 5-arch bridge at Tavistock, now demolished, crossed from behind St Rumon's School to the corner of Market Street; the old road jinked right then turned left along Duke Street. The main axis of the town was then north-south, whereas now it is east-west.

The modern A390 from Tavistock to Gunnislake is a fine example of the contortions needed by later turnpike engineers to provide a gentle gradient in our hilly landscape. An older route, now minor roads or RUPP, was far more direct.

But just where the evidence of an old straight line is most visible on the ground, Ogilby's map suggests two significant bends! Robert Morden in 1695, who probably had access to Ogilby's data, shows the direct route, though in a small-scale map, whilst Donn in 1765 is different again, showing a first generation turnpike turning right at Lumburn Bridge to Newton, then heading more or less directly for New Bridge. Perhaps a reader will be able to explain it to me!

…and at 27.2 pass the last direction stone on the right called Roundle. At 29.2 in a vale over a stone bridge of 2 arches you cross a brook, and 2 furlongs farther pass by 2 or 3 houses on the left called Merryvil, again crossing a brook at 30.3 where you descend a hill of 3 furlongs and leave the moor; whence over a stone bridge of 5 arches you cross the Tavy or Teave, enter Tavistock extending 4 furlongs on the road, but more transverse. It's a large well inhabited and frequented Borough town, formerly of great account for its abbey, which is now divided into tenements; it enjoys several immunities as sending burgesses to Parliament, etc, hath 2 almshouses, is well watered for through each street runs a small brook. It is governed by a portreeve and 8 magistrates, has a great market on Fridays, and 5 fairs annually; the Earl of Bedford being lord of the town.

Leaving Tavistock you cross a stone bridge of 2 arches over a brook at 34.7 and ascend a hill of 7 furlongs, at 36.4 in a vale you cross New Bridge of stone consisting of 6 fair arches over the River Tamer, and enter the county of Cornwall…

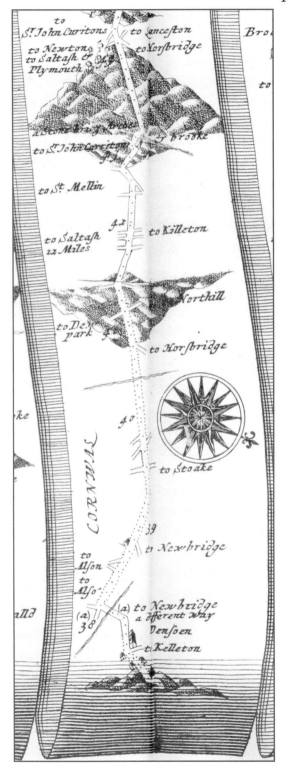

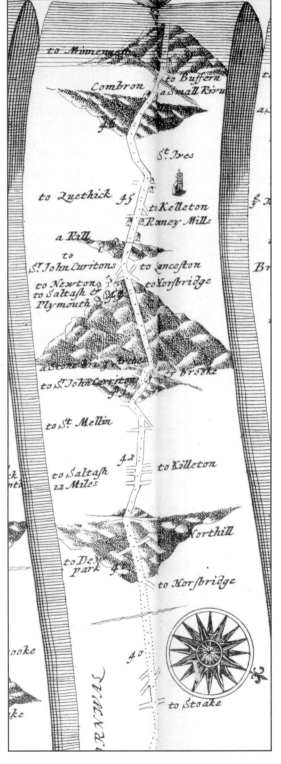

# Gunnislake - Callington

From New Bridge we take a bridle-way which, certainly at its top end, is a classic example of Ogilby road. It passes Lower Dimson Farm then, as a road, bears left to arrive at Higher Dimson. From here it either follows the track towards Delaware Farm or the road to the station. I imagine the 'different way' back on the left to Newbridge is by way of Hatches Green rather than by the present main road.

The route from Drakewalls to Callington broadly follows the A390.

The turning to 'Horsbridge' is probably at SX 380706, where there is still a highly distinctive old pillar indicating roads to Tavistock and Horsebridge. 'Dew Park' is Dupath and 'Killeton' is Callington. Did the old road follow today's by-pass (Southern Road) and then the bri-dleway through Pencrebar Farm?

Once across the Newbridge at 43.1 miles (like so many Cornish bridges, this one is fifteenth century new) two short cuts to the south of the A390 take us to St Ive. The right turns to Horsebridge and Launceston are a mystery, if they come as I think at SX 329678.

'Buffern' is presumably Butterdon (SX 294664).

7 furlongs beyond you pass by Denson a small village contiguous on the right, then passing over Henshaw Down at 40.6 you descend 6 furlongs, and at 42.6 descend again, and crossing a stone bridge of 3 arches, over a brook you ascend a hill of a mile in height; whence an easy descent by St Ives church on the right conveys you at 45.7 to a descent of 3 furlongs, at the bottom whereof you pass through Combrow a small village.

A furlong beyond you cross Combrow Water a small river…

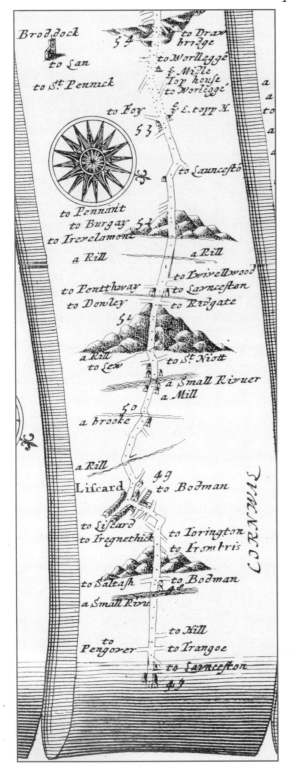

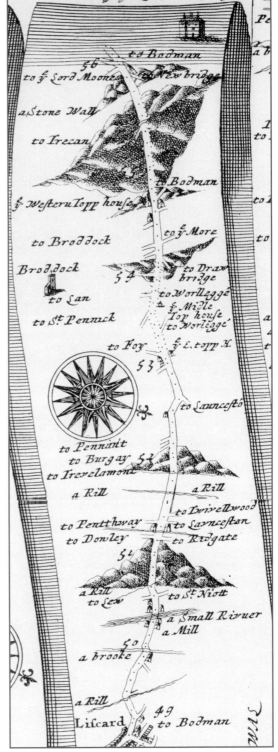

# Liskeard - Restormel

Presumably we follow A390 from Butterdon Mill to Liskeard, since Pengover lies to the left and 'Trombris' is Trembraze. A street plan of Liskeard reveals that the westward B3254 is New Road, whilst to the north of it is 'Old Road', running north of the school.

I assume Ogilby's 'Small Rivuer' is at Looe Mills, but how does he get there? By way of SX237647, or perhaps by SX237644, where an oddly curving field boundary joins a track?

We seem then to follow A38/A390 (though there is a line from Looe Mills consisting of lanes and one of those suggestive 'other routes with public access' running beside the railway track) to East Taphouse ('yᵉ E. topp H.') and 'yᵉ Western Topp house'.

'Lord Moon's' was Boconnoc. The 'New Bridge' is at SX129651. The section ends just beyond Fairy Cross.

...and ascend 4 furlongs and at the top pass through Merrymeet a small village, 7 furlongs farther you cross another small river, whence an easy ascent conveys you to Liscard or Liskerd, extending 3 furlongs on the road, but more transvers; it is situate in a level, and had formerly a castle, now ruinous; is an indifferent large Town Corporate, driving a considerable trade in yarn, which is vended at Exeter, etc; it enjoys several immunities as sending burgesses to Parliament etc, has a good free school; is governed by a Mayor, Recorder, 6 Magistrates, etc, has a good market on Saturdays and 5 fairs annually.

From Liscard you pass over several ascents and descents and pass over several small waters or rills, and by the Eastern, Middle and Western Taphouses; leaving Broddock church on the left and Lestormy Castle on the right which is now ruinous, but was formerly the seat of the Dukes of Cornwall, and commanded Listwithiel near adjoining;

*Restormel Castle in picturesque ruin*

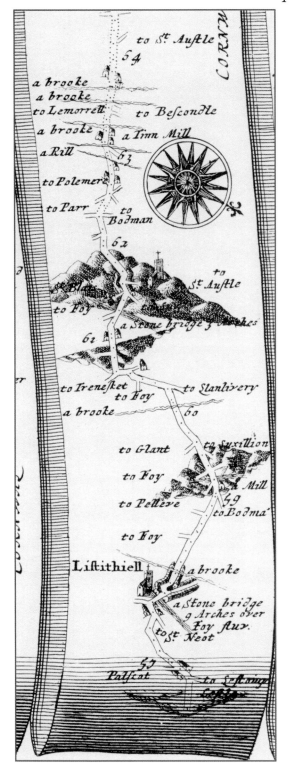

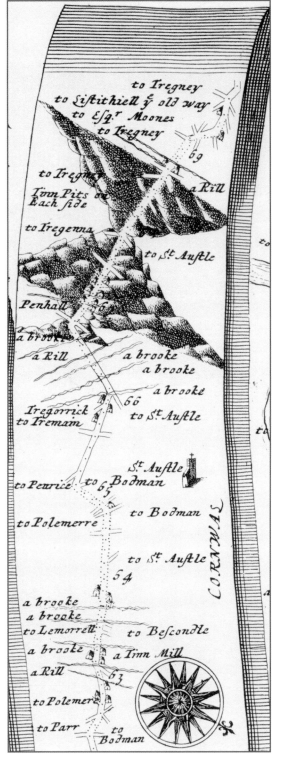

It appears that, at the milestone south of Fairy Cross, the old road bears right joining a lane past the disused quarry, then left into Polscoe ('Palscat') and right across the old bridge into Lostwithiel.

The A390 makes a steep ascent out of the town, but the old road past the cemetery is steeper. A390 is followed to Penpillick.

At St Blazey we have to cross the river by an early 16th century bridge, now gone, and pass to the left of the church, which suggests a route along 'Driving Lane'; this certainly has the typical character of an Ogilby road. From Gascoyne, it appears that the old bridge was at SX070549.

We then seem to follow, approximately, A390. The tin mill was perhaps near Wheal Eliza Consols, opposite the garden centre.

Compare 28C for the route to and through Tregorrick. From Tregorrick it is guesswork. Perhaps unlike 28C we go to London Apprentice, then through Little Polgooth and Lower Sticker to Hewas Water where there is a complex of road junctions. This is certainly the only route offered by Gascoyne in 1699, but that is no proof against travellers having taken a more direct route 25 years earlier, especially since this was at the time one of Cornwall's most active mining areas – a fast changing landscape.

…then passing through Polsco a small village at 56.7 you 7 furlongs farther over a stone bridge of 9 arches cross the Foy and enter Listwithiel, in Cornish Lest-Uthiel, by Ptolemy Uzella, formerly seated on a hill but now in a bottom; and it was of greater account than now it is, the river being choked up; it is at present a Town Corporate, enjoying several privileges as sending burgesses to Parliament, hath a share in the coinage of the tin, is the only place where the goal [sic] and courts for the Stannary are kept; is governed by a Mayor etc, enjoying a good market on Fridays.

From Listwithiel you again cross several hills and waters, and pass through St Blais at 61.4, Tregorrick at 66 miles, and Polebooth at 67.1 all small villages;

---

'We crossed Par Bay to Par, a small key and harbour near St Blazey. Here we first saw a streamwork of tin, that is, of tin stone and tin grains wash'd down to the bottom from the lodes or veins…

We came to a little tinning town called St Austle, partly built of more stone [moorstone] or granite, and partly of a free stone which they find to the south-south-west. We went up the hill and struck out of the way to the south, to other tin works called Pool-gooth, where they have a fire engine, and on the other side of the vale are Lord Edgcomb's works.'

Dr Richard Pococke, 1750

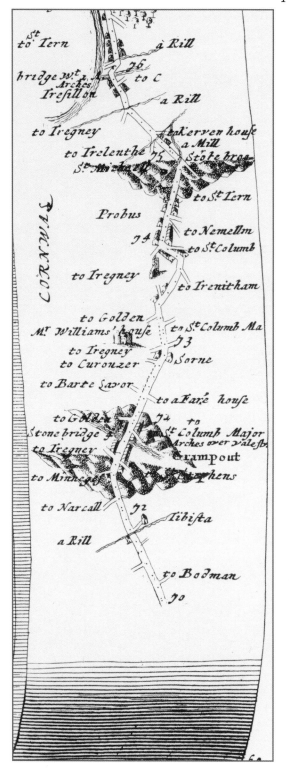

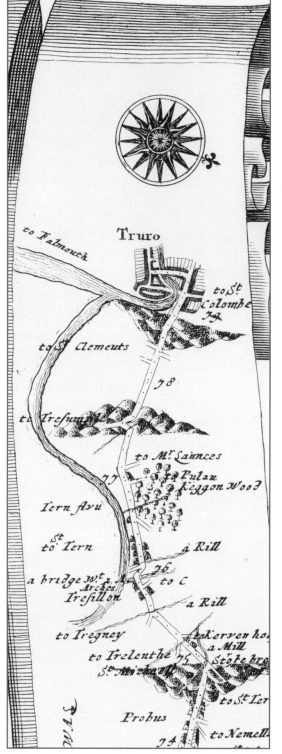

# Grampound - Truro

We start on A390 somewhere near Penans (SW954490). 'Tibista' has disappeared (except for a street name within Grampound), but I wonder if the bridleway once extended from SW948487 to the Town Mills? If so, 'Tibista' could have been where that bridleway turns at right angles.

After Grampound, the route presumably follows the bridleway just north of Carvossa ('Curouzer') and Mr Williams' house (Trewithen?): I cannot identify 'Sorne' which seems to be at SW920483. Then we pick up the line of the old A390 into Probus and on to Tresillian. It carried straight on at Kiggon, up a steep wooded hill and past Penair School, descending into Truro by St Clements Hill.

When, in 1825 the Truro Turnpike Trust was negotiating with William Macadam, they said that they wanted 'to save sufficient [on maintenance costs] to expend in an alteration and improvement of our line of road; which from its partial steepness and narrowness, is very defective.'

Presumably the present A390 from Tregolls Road to Pencalenick was one of the subsequent improvements.

One interesting road, now B3275 from Fraddon to Tresillian, dates from the late eighteenth century; its curves and gradients are beautifully designed for coach and horses – and for cars at modest speeds – and it makes an interesting contrast to the holloways of Ogilby's time.

…whence you enter Grampond or Grampont at 71.3 seated on the small River Valle. A Town Corporate, sends burgesses to Parliament; is governed by a Mayor, Recorder and 8 Magistrates, it contains about 100 houses, is in the parish of Creed, has a market on Tuesdays and 2 fairs yearly.

Whence passing through Sorne at 72.7, Probus at 74 miles, and Tresillon at 75.5 all small villages, you enter Truro at 78.7 a large and well frequented Corporation and market town (see page 85).

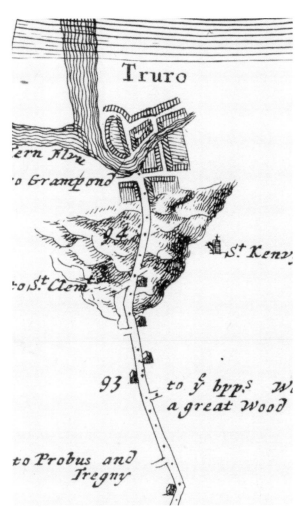

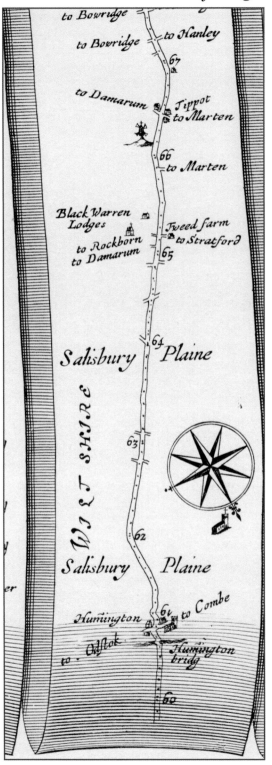

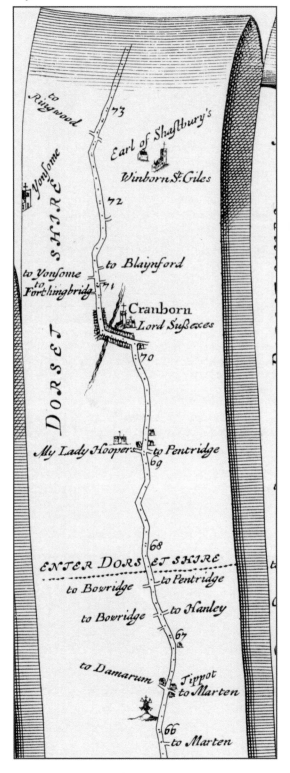

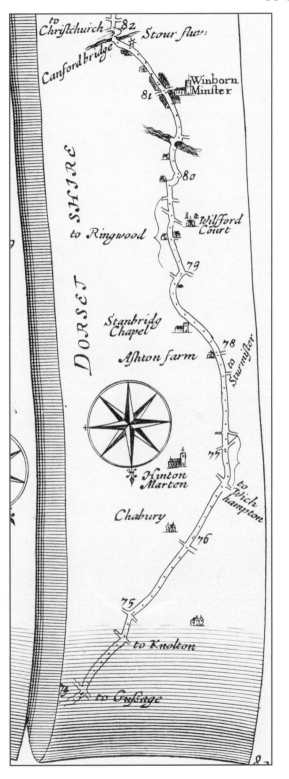

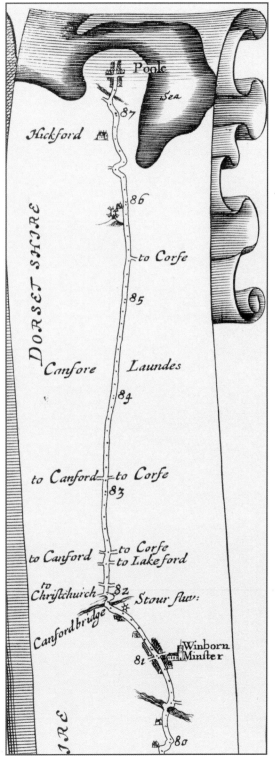

# The road from Exeter to Dorchester

*The road in most places, though something hilly, affords an indifferent good way,
and handsome entertainment in the towns and other
places you pass through.*

## 94A    OS Explorer sheets 114 and 115

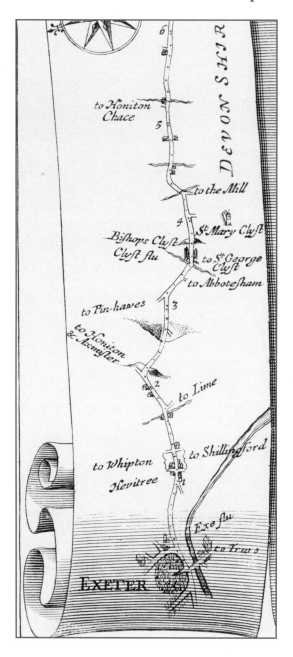

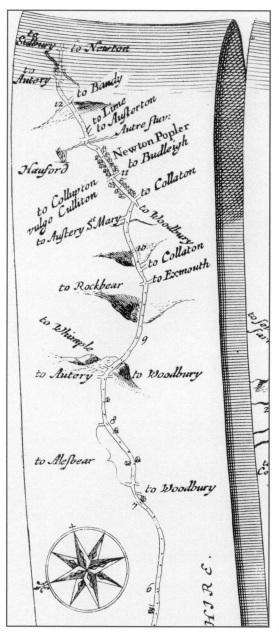

# Exeter - Newton Poppleford

Perhaps more than any other of the routes involving Exeter, this brings home the difference in size of the modern city. We leave Exeter by Magdalen Street and Magdalen Road, then Heavitree Road – but, if the map is to be believed, we leave the built-up area when we reach the city wall, now with its pedestrian bridge.

In Heavitree we bear right into Quarry Lane (at SX947922 if you are using the OS map) which becomes Sidmouth Road past the Park & Ride. We pick it up again beyond the M5 with the splendid long bridge over the Clyst, pass through the village of Bishops Clyst, now scarcely to be distinguished from Clyst St Mary, and join the A3052. The crossroads with ways to 'Autery' and Woodbury will be at the Half-way Inn (B3180).

Once across the Ottery at Newton Poppleford, 'Austerton' must be Otterton.

What exactly happens next, I don't know! Is the Lyme turning the present Four Elms Hill, then Greenway Lane? Or was this junction at SY101896, with Greenway Lane as the main route and the Lyme road taking a more southern route? It seems improbable.

Setting forward from the City of Exeter, the account of which you have seen in the road from London to the Lands End (page 33). At 1.1 you pass through Hevitre a small village, and by some scattering houses, and a small ascent and descent, are brought at 3.5 to Bishops Clyst, first crossing the River Clyst, which leaving, you ascend a small hill, and pass by St Mary Clyst on the right; then again by several dispersed houses, and crossing several small waters or rills, and by an ascent and 2 descents, are brought at 10.6 to Newton Poppler, a long but discontinued village of 5 furlongs extent; at the end whereof you cross the Autre, and leave Hauford church on the left;

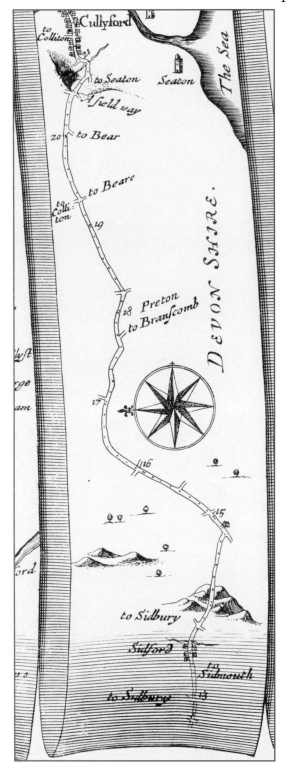

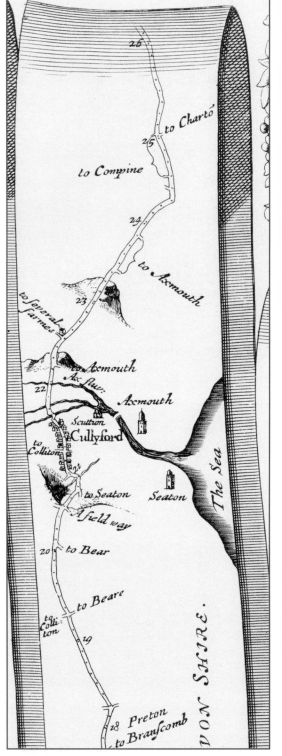

# Sidford - Lyme

We follow the A 3052 through Sidford. The Sidbury turning, coming after the river, must be that from Steven's Cross. An older route is evident at the top of the hill, and the sharp change of direction is clearly at Trow Farm. From here, as Ogilby says, little presents itself and we follow A 3052, though without the abrupt change of direction at Manor Farm, descending Harepath Hill (the name suggesting a Saxon main road) to a junction at SY 244920 where a road leads back on the right to Seaton.

We enter Colyford and cross (then) three branches of the Axe. Axmouth could then claim to be a port town, perhaps the successor of Roman Moridunum. The A358 did not exist. Combpyne was accessible by the footpath from Heathfield Cross.

On the next sheet we enter Lyme, though if we want to go to Bridport, we can follow Clappentail Lane, Roman Road and Colway Lane rather than descending into the town.

…then ascending and crossing a rill, you are conveyed at 13.4 through a small village called Sidford, a little beyond which you ascend 2 furlongs, and at 14.6 bear to the left, little presenting itself till at 20.4 you descend 3 furlongs, and crossing a rill, enter Cullyford a disunited village of 5 furlongs extent; at the end of which you cross 3 separated branches of the Ax, not far from its influx into the sea, and pass within one mile of Axmouth a small port-town on the right, and Scuttum House some distance upon the same hand.

Hence an irregular road over 2 ascents brings you at 27 miles to a descent of 6 furlongs, at the bottom whereof you cross a small river, and at once enter Dorsetshire and Lime or Lime Regis, a large and well built town extending 5 furlongs on the road, is seated near the sea and on a good and well known haven. It's a Corporation and market town, governed by a Mayor, etc, sends burgesses to Parliament, and is a place of good traffic, its privileges being granted by Edward the Third.

Whence the sea accompanies you near the road on the right for several miles together, and bearing to the left, are brought at 30 miles to enter Shaderson a village of 3 furlongs extent; and 3 furlongs beyond the town, leaving the church on the left, to cross Steymag Bridge over a small river; then by Stanton Gabriel church on the right, and some dispersed houses on the road, come at 34.5 to Chiddiok a village of 3 furlongs; and at 36.7 (first leaving Sinsborow church on the left) to Bridport alias Birtport or Bruteport, a place not large, yet seated between 2 small rivers, near their influx into the sea. It's a Corporation and market town, sending burgesses to Parliament, and is governed by 2 Bailiffs, etc and was formerly the only place for the twisting of cordage for the Navy Royal of England.

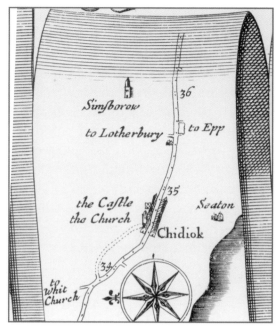

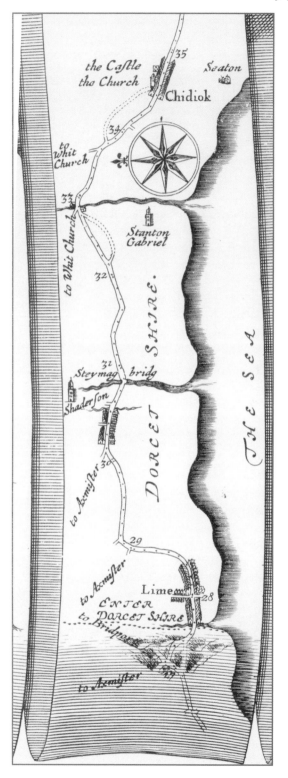

At the end of Bridport you cross Allington Bridge; whence an indifferent straight way by Waldich and Lytton churches on the right, and long Lother and Askatham on the left, brings you at 46.7 to a village of 2 furlongs extent; little else occurring till at 51.5 you enter Dorchester, a town of great antiquity, being a station of the Romans; is pleasantly situated on the Froom and on the Foss Way; is the chief town in the county, large and well built, containing 3 parish churches; is a Corporation governed by 2 Bailiffs, a Recorder, 8 Aldermen, etc. Sends burgesses to Parliament, and as being the shire town, is the place where the Assizes are kept for the county. It hath a good free school and an almshouse, and is dignified by giving title to the Right Honourable Henry Pierpoint Marquess of Dorchester, etc, and its market which is on Saturdays is well stored with all sorts of provisions.

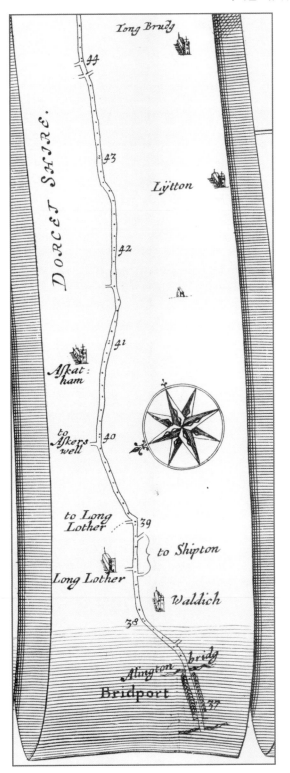

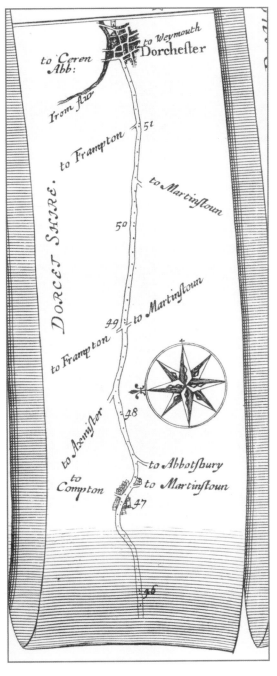

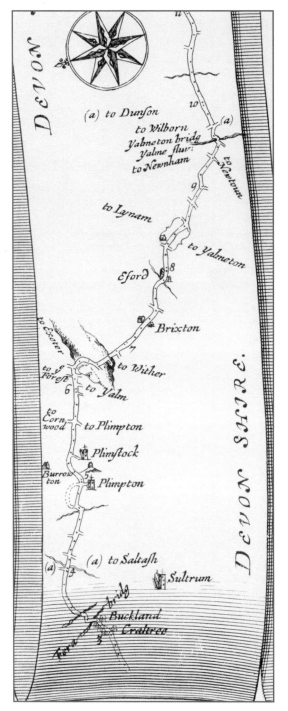

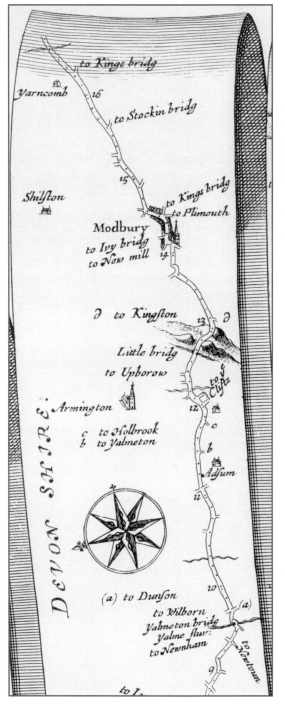

We leave Plymouth by B3214 through Lipson Vale, with Efford on our left, crossing the Plym by 'Fera Bridge' at Marsh Mills. Then we take B3416, leaving it to follow Ridgeway through Plympton. (Does the surveyor misinterpret Plympton St Maurice as Plymstock?)

What happens next is rather surprising: at SX561555 we take an abrupt leave of the Exeter road and follow the curve of Deep Lane (which on the ground seems like a twentieth century highway engineer's plan but is apparently ancient) and then bear left (the turning has been sanitised by the highway engineers after all: you can't escape them) down past EffordFarm, Lyneham and Yeo Park to 'Yalmeton bridg'. (The mention of Brixton in Ogilby is utterly misleading, though of course we are in Brixton parish.)

'Adsum' is presumably Addistone, and the 'Upburow' (Ugborough) road is presumably not A3121 but the lesser road parallel to it to the south, which (significantly?) forms the 'Co Const Bdy'. Do we now cross Goutsford Bridge and take the track beside Aylestone Brook?

Within Modbury, we leave the modern main road and turn left up B3207 passing Stokenbridge to the south and Yarnacombe to the north, to Brownston.

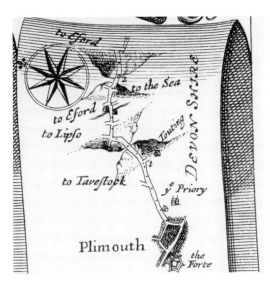

From Plymouth (page 41) you pass 2 ascents and descents, and at 3 miles pass through Buckland Craltree a small village, where you cross Fera Bridge over a brook, and after by Sultrum, Plimpton (which sendeth burgesses to Parliament, and hath a small market on Saturdays) and Plimstock churches all on the right, and Burrowton House on the left, and at 6.5 cross a vale; thence passing by some houses on the road called Brixton and Eford, you at 9.5 over Yalm Bridge cross the Yalm, and passing by Adsum House on the right, and Armington church some distance on the left, and 12.6 you ascend an hill of 2 furlongs, and at 14.1 enter Modbury a town of 4 furlongs extent, seated between 2 hills in a bottom, and hath an indifferent market on Saturdays.

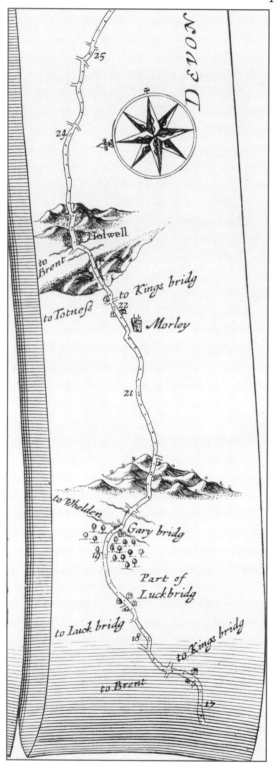

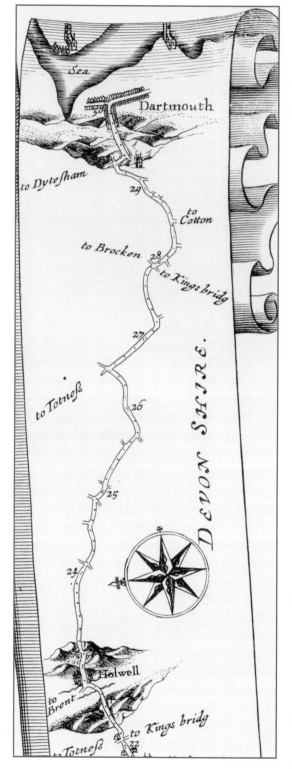

# Modbury - Dartmouth

We start at approximately SW 700528 and go through California Cross, south of Lupridge ('Luckbridg') to Gara Bridge. We then climb, I think, to High Marks Barn on our way to Moreleigh, dropping down in Halwell, where we shimmy left and right up to Halwell Cross and the A3122. Ogilby's Kingsbridge-Totnes road crosses our route not at Halwell church, as today, but at Moreleigh Cross (SW 767528).

The A381 through Halwell is presumably a later improvement: in which case the branch 'to Brent' is either mis-named or is the track to Boreston; there is the hint of a lost track across the fields to Horner Tongue, from which there is indeed a lane through Diptford to Brent.

From Halwell, we follow the present A3122, including the abrupt change of direction at the Sportsman's Arms. How convenient it would be if the turn 'to Totness' was still a practicable route! But it is far easier to brave the jams on the main road than to try this ancient short cut.

The present main road into Dartmouth plays havoc with the old street plan. The route must (I conjecture from Ogilby and Donn rather than from local knowledge) have gone either down Mount Boone and Ridge Hill, or down Townstal Hill and Clarence Hill.

Hence by Shilston and Yarncomb Houses some distance to the left, and several dispersed houses on the road, through Luckbridg a small village at 18.4 and through a wood, cross Gary Bridge, and leave the church on the right; and ascending 3 furlongs pass by Morley church on the right at 21.6 and through Holwel a village at 22.7; seated in a large vale; whence an irregular road brings you at 29.3 to a descent, at the bottom whereof you enter Dartmouth, a market and port town (see page 105).

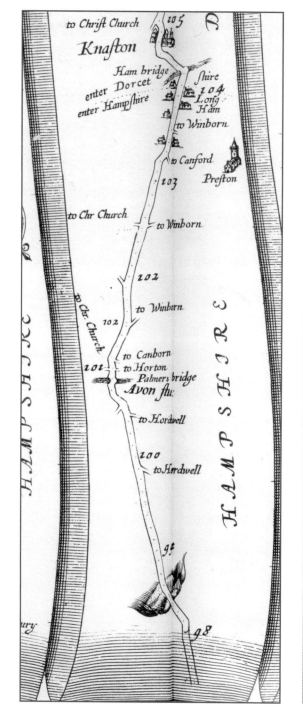

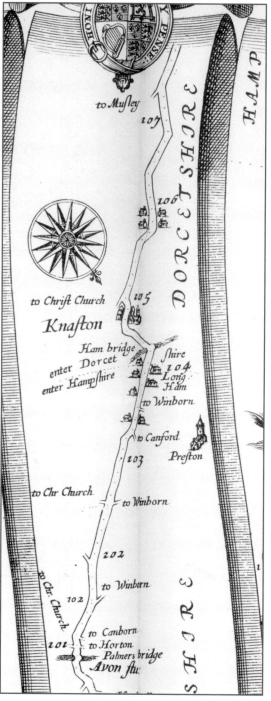

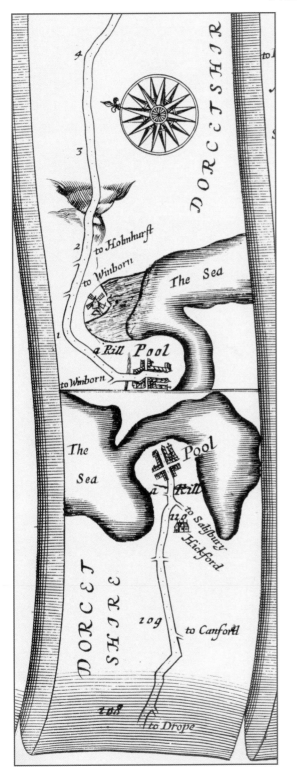

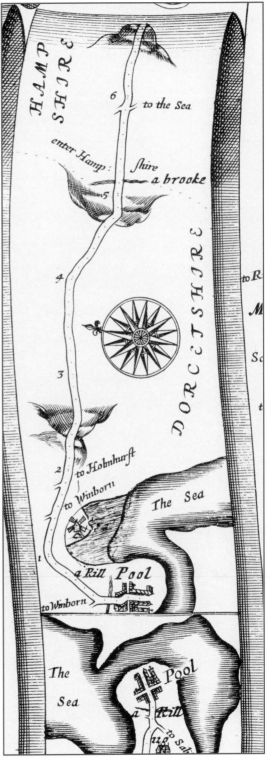

# Index of people and places

Where a place appears in the text opposite a map on the facing page, only the text page is listed in the index.